D1634031

Rock
Gardening

Rock
Gardening

WITHDRAWN
From Swindon
Borough Libraries

ROY GENDERS

O O16748 OO

1 852890

635.9672

JOHN GIFFORD LTD
LONDON

SBN 0 7071 0004 6

John Gifford Ltd
125 Charing Cross Road
London, W.C.2

First published 1955
Reprinted March 1959

© *W. & G. Foyle Ltd., 1959*

This revised edition published by John Gifford Ltd, 1973

Text set in Times Roman and
printed in Great Britain by the Hope Burgess Group
on Tudor Coated Cartridge. Bound by
James Burn Bookbinders Ltd, Esher

Contents

PART I

Contents continued

PART II

Rock and water garden

PART I

1   Value of the Rockery in the Modern Garden

Utilizing the smallest space – More suggestions – Selecting a
site – Use of alpine plants without stone – A profitable hobby.

We live in an age of small gardens with the compact garden of
the town house now taking the place of the rambling but
conventional garden of the country estate, and so it is necessary
to utilize space to the best advantage and at the same time to
grow those plants which will provide as long a flowering

period as possible, with the minimum of attention. There is a wide selection of plants for the rockery which will provide colour all the year round, even during the darkest days of winter, and by careful planning it will be possible to make a rockery in almost any garden, no matter how difficult its shape, or how restricted for space, a mass of colour throughout the year.

The small town garden cannot be planted with trees and bulbs and be expected to look like a real woodland garden, for to obtain a completely natural effect, space is necessary. A rock garden, however, may so be planted that it will give a natural effect even in the most confined spaces and the range of plants is so extensive that no matter what the soil and situation, there should be a display of interest and colour all the year round. In the more exposed gardens of the North where one may find some difficulty in obtaining a colourful display from the herbaceous border or from bedding schemes, a rock garden will provide colour through every season, for it must be remembered that not only will the plants receive some valuable protection from the judiciously placed rockery stones, but very many of the plants used will have been introduced from the mountains of the Himalayas or the Andes and will be happier only under cool conditions.

Utilizing the smallest space

Even the smallest space may be made colourful; a corner of a yard where the walls cast their shadows and look anything but attractive can be quite easily and permanently transformed into a most delightful rock garden. One of the most pleasing small gardens I ever saw was made in the backyard of a West Country cottage. The front door opened on to the road and so only at the back of the cottage was space available. A low wall surrounded the yard which was paved with cut stone. Between the two side walls and completely hiding the wall at the end of the yard, the rockery had been made with natural Westmorland stone. It did not give the appearance that the stone had been tipped from a lorry like so many rock gardens do, but the stone had been carefully and tastefully placed in layers, which gave the appearance of the stone in its natural surroundings; in fact, the stone itself was quite inconspicuous, which is as it should be. It had been planted to provide as prolonged a display of colour as space would permit, and rarely was it devoid of at least some colour throughout the year. Even during January, when black frost hardened the soil, the rockery was protected by the stones and the low walls surrounding it, and on days when the rays of the winter sun shone through the clouds, the butterfly blooms of the hardy winter cyclamen and of *Crocus imperati* and Polyanthus Barrowby Gem, were to be seen from the back windows of the house.

Or another small rockery I recall, was made at the end of a long garden at the point where two high walls joined. Silver birch trees with their colourful bark hid much of the walling, but a dark corner was made most colourful by using rich red sandstone to make a rockery and planting it almost entirely with small evergreens. Here the accent was on keeping the rockery tidy with the minimum of attention, which will not be easy if too many plants are crowded together and especially if trailing plants are used. Small bulbs which will die back after flowering and permit easy clearing, dwarf evergreens, and plants of a compact habit like the saxifrages, should be used where gardening time is at a minimum, for nothing looks more unattractive than a rockery which has become a wilderness through neglect.

An original suggestion is to utilize a grass covered bank by cutting away the turf and soil, to insert the stones. Bulbs may be planted in the grass in great variety and which, if carefully chosen, will provide an all year round display and will look most charming in their natural surroundings. Here the only attention the rockery will need, will be to keep the stones free from untidy grass by cutting it back around the stones two or three times a year.

More suggestions

Again, a dry wall used to divide the fruit or vegetable garden from a lawn can be made most colourful by planting trailing rock plants amongst the stones. Or a path may be brought to life by the use of crazy paving, using carpeting plants to provide the colour. Where space is even more restricted than in the town garden, a tiny rock garden may be made in a window box or in a stone trough, or in a narrow border beneath a window. But in each of these three places the stone must be used in the same tasteful way to give the appearance of natural rock, rather than of stones thrown together by children on the sea shore.

The rock garden came into vogue during the early years of the twentieth century to counteract the straight lines of Georgian and Victorian gardens. It was, so to speak, a revolt against the era of Le Notre and Capability Brown and of the formality of the Victorian garden, but the rockery soon became its own enemy for stones were thrown together in too precise heaps and with little thought given to selection of a suitable position. The specialist rock garden constructors of the present day are endeavouring to educate us in this respect and nowhere is their work seen to better advantage than at the Southport Show each year, where the high bank, backed by evergreen and ornamental trees, acts as a pleasing contrast to the cascading rockeries and waterfalls, so ably planted with drifts of flowering plants which in a few days are made to appear as if they had been there from the beginning of time.

Selecting a site   The rock garden, of whatever proportions, should strike the happy medium. As Reginald Farrer has said: 'the rock garden must have a plan', it should possess neither the conventional stiffness of the Victorian garden nor the chaos of a volcanic eruption. Nature has a purpose and so must the rockery. Care should be taken in selecting a site which will provide as natural a condition as possible; a bank, a dell, a gully or planted against a wall are all positions which will provide a suitable rock garden. Not only in selecting a site, but in the formation of the rockery itself, progress but slowly until things appear clear to one's mind; in other words, work to a plan. Whereas the Japanese have been masters of the rock garden for a thousand years, we are only just beginning to understand the rudiments of gardening with stone and alpine plants, which is no less an art than the formation of the natural garden, or laying out a garden on formal lines, at both of which we excel.

10

Value of the Rockery in the Modern Garden

The rockery must be constructed to conform with the lie of one's land and though one may wish for the rockery to be constructed in some particular position, it will be much more satisfactory to work to the more natural lie of the ground, for this will be half-way to success. A good position will make the construction of the rockery a relatively easy matter, but should there be no natural slope then this must be man-made which is far more difficult to do. For the land to lend itself to the making of a rockery with a natural and inconspicuous appearance, as if made by nature, will call for all one's ingenuity.

Before commencing the rockery, a visit to the limestone regions of Westmorland, North Yorkshire or Cheddar will enable one to see the rock formation in its natural state. One will be amazed by strata or layers of rock of varying thicknesses yet with the grain running exactly in the same direction, thus showing no sign of having been clumped together as do so many man-made rockeries. So few give any thought to this and even if only a conglomeration of garden stones are being employed, it will be most important to construct them in layers to give the impression of continuation, rather than to stick them into a mound of soil without any relation to the natural formation of rocks. Where it is not possible to visit these natural rock garden areas, try to obtain as many photographs as possible showing the use of various stones in natural formation, for only by the careful study of rock formation will it be possible to construct a rockery on the correct natural lines.

It is not necessary to employ large quantities of stone in order to enjoy a garden of alpine plants. A most interesting collection of plants may be formed by using concrete flagstones, leaving small pockets for soil as the work of laying the stone progresses, or a piece of rough land may be so planted on natural lines that it will give the appearance of an alpine meadow. Having a flat piece of land on which there were several large boulders, said to have been used by ancient man to mark land for direction purposes, I planted dwarf cupressus trees in variety and a wide selection of bulbs to be found under natural conditions. The effect was one of great beauty and I am sure was a far more

The use of alpine plants without stone

11

successful use of this flat piece of land than if I had attempted to use large quantities of stone to create a quite unnatural effect. Again, study one's land, then form a plan. A delightful rockery may be made by using a small amount of stone at the sides of stone steps, the steps being the focal point of the particular ground and may be planted up the sides with all manner of lovely alpine plants. But for lending a more natural effect to a formal garden and for bringing the maximum colour to the smallest of gardens, the judicious use of stone and the wide range of alpine plants are worthy of the utmost consideration in the modern garden.

A profitable hobby

As there is always a large demand for rock plants, it may be worthy of thought as to the construction of a rockery in one's garden with a view to building up a profitable hobby in the sale of plants. Some small pots in a cold frame would be required, but the outlay would not be excessive and planting could at first be confined to those popular plants of easy propagation and culture, such as rock roses (Helianthemum) and various saxifrages, primulas and dianthus (Alpine Pinks). I commenced a large nursery business in the 1930's in exactly this way. Answering an advertisement from a firm of contractors in Bournemouth for rock plants of every description, I was able to clear the whole of the large 50′ long frame at a profitable figure and was on the road to a successful business. To-day, the demand is even greater, for only now is the rockery coming into its own, for it is just the thing for the modern garden of restricted space.

2   Selecting and Placing the Stone

Ideal rockery stone – Limestone – Sandstone – Using the
stone – Making a start – Employ only natural stones.

It is agreed that a rockery should be constructed as naturally
as it is possible, so that it will give the appearance of having
been placed in position without any attention from man. There
are also the plants to consider and most alpines possess a deep
rooting system and are lovers of a cool, moist soil. This is
essential to a flourishing plant and so it is necessary to provide
the roots with stone which goes deep into the soil and which
will encourage the roots to creep along in search of moisture.
Rockery stone must not only be pleasing to the eye but must
have depth so that the portion out of the ground can give
protection from strong sun and winds, and the portion under
the soil can provide the roots with moisture and cool conditions.
It is said that the ideal rock garden stone should have two-thirds
of its form beneath the soil and only one-third exposed; that
stone which does not penetrate to sufficient depth will play but
little part in the rooting system of the alpine plant. Far too
many rockeries are seen with stones merely pressed into the top
few inches of the soil where they afford little help to the rooting
system of the plants.

Limestone

The limestone of Westmorland, the result of thousands of
years of weathering in the action of air and water, is not only
pleasing to the eye on account of its rugged, natural form, but
being composed of compressed billions of calcerous forms of
insect life, the roots of the plants are able to penetrate deep into
the stone itself, thus receiving the cool conditions so essential
to a healthy alpine plant. Again, the limestone is so weathered
as to be composed of cracks and crevices and holes of varying
sizes and shapes which, when filled with soil, make up a minia-

ture garden in themselves. For a rockery then, there is no stone equal to that of North Country limestone, which may be so easily set in layers and which never gives the impression of having been dumped. Its colour is also far easier to harmonize with richly coloured alpines than that of any other stone. It is made up of layers of every shade of grey and white which blend with the blues and scarlets like no other colouring. This stone is removed from the hills and mountains where it lies exposed to the elements; it is not quarried in the same way as sandstone and granite. It is soft and possesses a beauty of natural colour, whether used for a water garden built up a bank, or merely used as a low terrace with almost no fall to show the colouring of the stone to its greatest advantage. But as weathered and natural as limestone is, it will demand the same treatment in the construction of the rockery as any other stone, the stone being tilted at the same angle and matching in grain as near as possible. A more natural effect is provided by using stone of much the same size so that there are no boulders surrounded by a number of tiny stones, but rather tiers or layers of stone of much the same height above soil level.

Sandstone   Those who live in the Midlands and the South and who may wish to use stone from a local quarry will be advised to use

14   *Nemophila menziesii*

Bellis perennis fl.pl.

red sandstone where possible. True, it possesses the disadvantage of being rather too rectangular, but by careful construction of the rockery, it will be possible to overcome this by varying the heights above ground to a greater degree than if limestone is used.

One well-known specialist has stated that sandstone blocks always look 'isolated and imported' and yet one of the loveliest of all moraine gardens I ever saw was built of sandstone and especially was its warm colour appreciated during winter-time. Carefully constructed, it never gave the appearance of looking artificial, for the stone crumbles when exposed to the elements and soon loses its sharp edges. Not so granite and Portland stone which, though beautifully coloured, is hard and sharp edged and takes a considerable time to weather. A compromise is obtained from the rich, soft yellow Cotswold Stone which is perhaps more commonly used than any other, but too large an area should not appear out of the soil or the effect will be severe and artificial instead of being soft and natural as obtained from the use of weathered limestone.

It must be remembered that not all rock gardens are of the same size and the size of the stone should be in proportion to the size of the garden or rockery. If the rockery is to be very small then the stone should be cut to scale, for nothing looks worse than a small rockery composed of just one or two huge 15 stones; likewise, nothing looks more unnatural than the use of very small stones to form a rockery of large proportions or in a large garden. Again, the stone should be all of one type. Mixed stone will look quite out of place however skilfully it is used.

Using the stone   Having obtained the stone and to the required size, the work of construction should proceed slowly, each piece of stone being carefully placed into position depending upon the contour of the site. Some believe that the more quickly and roughly the work is done, the more natural will be the effect. This is not so, for usually the finished rockery gives only the appearance of having been shot from a lorry. As far as possible the stones should match those nearest each other in size and form and this can only be achieved if the stones are carefully selected as the work proceeds. It may be necessary to turn a stone several times before the correct position is achieved. The best effect is obtained if the flat side or surface is left exposed, for again this is the more natural rock formation. A rock garden with dozens of pointed stones, like pagodas in a Malayan jungle, will look quite unnatural, for no stones are ever weathered by nature in this way.

If it is intended to make the rockery on a bank or sloping ground, all small and ill-shapen stone may be used for making the foundation at the base. This will serve a twofold purpose. It will help to make a solid foundation and will also provide additional moisture and coolness around which the roots of the plants may penetrate. Pieces of limestone are especially useful in this way, for being of a porous nature the roots will easily penetrate to the centre of the stones which are always cool and moist. The same seeking out for moisture and cool conditions may be observed amongst paths of crazy paving stones, the soil beneath the stones becoming a tangled mass of web-like root threads which may even penetrate into the grain of the stones causing them to split.

To ensure that the maximum amount of moisture reaches the plants, overhanging stone should not be allowed unless it be just one such stone beneath which a plant such as *Primula*

16

edgworthii, may seek protection from excess moisture during the winter. The surface of the stones should slope in a slightly downward position to enable the maximum amount of moisture to reach the plants set in the shelter of the stones. The stones should be set as far as possible to afford the plants protection against prevailing winds which might, in a dry period, cause the newly-planted alpines to dry out and become wind-scorched which may take them considerable time to recover.

Where to start in the construction of the rockery often calls for thought, and occasionally causes some difficulty. Where building is being done on ground with a sharp slope, it is better to commence at the bottom and work up the slope and the commencement presents no difficulty. Where constructing on a more level site which has to be artificially raised, the contour should be carefully considered before laying the first stone. This stone should be the key to the whole scheme and care must be given to place it in a position around which the whole rockery may be constructed. The distance showing above the soil, the grain which it is desired to use for the whole rockery, the angle of the stones, the need to place in the correct position so as to afford shelter from the prevailing winds must all be taken into consideration whilst this first stone is being set.

Making a start

It may be required to work in a scree composed of finely broken stone in which some of the saxifrages and dianthus plants are happiest and this should be placed between two main ridges of rock or formed in a pocket made between wall or path and ridge. I am a great advocate of using scree as much as possible about the rockery and especially if sandstone is being used. The contrast caused by the use of washed gravel for the scree is most pleasing, whilst the gravel contributes greatly to keeping down weeds and giving the rockery a tidy appearance. 'Tufa' rock for a scree is also excellent and especially if used in conjunction with weathered limestone to which it is similar, though unlike limestone it contains vegetable matter which has become stone-like in character. It is excellent for encouraging root action, but having a high lime content the selection of plants should be in general confined to those having an appetite for lime.

Some consideration should always be given to the use of stone which most nearly resembles that from which have been built the house and outbuildings. Where local sandstone has originally been used for building construction then sandstone should be used to make the rockery. But since Elizabethan days sandstone has only been infrequently used, yet it blends with brick exceptionally well, as does limestone with the white-washed walls of a cottage. Where Cotswold stone is used for building construction, then the same may be used with charm to build the rock garden. All that is well worth some consideration, for it must be remembered that the rockery will remain as long as will the house and garden where it is constructed, though the plants may be changed from time to time, depending upon whether they flourish or not. I once used the large sandstone from an old wall with very great effect. The wall had been built at the same time as the house and so was equally weathered and fitted into the scheme of garden and home to the utmost advantage. This is what the rockery should do, for after all, just as a terrace is an integral part of a house, so should be the rockery.

Spar stone, shining white in colour and with rough pointed edges, is sometimes used for rockery construction. This always seems to be quite out of tune both with the alpine plants to be set around it and with the garden in general. I am much against using any stone that does not blend with its surroundings, and I have never yet seen spar stone to look happy. In the same way, the use of various ornaments about the rockery is to be deplored, and those mixtures of pixies and mushrooms, often in the most gaudy colourings, never look natural on a rockery. After all, who ever saw such objects halfway up the Himalayas or even on Helvellyn? It is our object to make the rock garden as natural in all its forms as is possible with the material to hand.

A Kentish rock garden

3 Making the Rockery

Importance of drainage – Preparing the soil – Climatic conditions – Setting the stones – Scree conditions – The water rockery.

Having carefully selected the position and type of stone to be used, the construction of the rock garden and preparation of the soil will be the next consideration. Where the rockery is to be constructed on an almost level site the need for ample drainage is of the utmost importance. If the soil is of a dry nature, as much boiler ash or broken brick or stone rubble as possible should be worked in. It may even be better to remove the soil over the whole area to a depth of about 12″ and to add a thick layer of clinker or crushed brick or stone before replacing much of the soil.

If the ground is at all low lying and in a rainy district, this will be well worth the extra effort entailed. Rock plants insist on thorough drainage and a well-nourished soil, for it must be remembered that they are most often found growing on high ground where drainage is almost perfect and the roots of the plants are able to penetrate into the rich alluvial deposits formed in the cracks of the rocks over many years. There the plants receive food, moisture and the cool conditions which they so much enjoy, whilst at the same time drainage material is completely adequate.

Having placed the drainage material into the excavated ground, this should be covered with a layer of rotted turf or with any other porous material available; decayed leaves, bracken or straw will be suitable and will provide additional drainage. Then over this place the soil must be made as porous and as fertile as possible. This is much easier to do than to improve the soil when once the plants are established. If the soil is on the heavy side, then a liberal amount of coarse sand should be incorporated and some peat or leaf mould is indispensable. I prefer to add this to the soil as the laying of the stones progresses and the compost is packed in the pockets made by the stones. But before any stones are laid, see that drainage is complete, for if there is anything that plants detest, it is to have their roots in a stagnant soil which is a very different thing than a cool, moist soil. Into the soil add coarse sand, some finely crushed brick if thought necessary and some peat and this will be the base into which the stones are to be set.

Preparing the soil

For filling up the cracks and pockets into which the plants are to be planted, a richer and more carefully prepared soil should be made up. If the soil is of poor quality, possibly excessively alkaline or one which has become too acid with city soot deposits, this should be dressed with lime after its acid content has first been tested, the amount of lime depending upon the degree of acidity. If the soil is stiff with excess clay, as much wood ash as possible should be worked in, or it may be thought necessary to obtain some sandy loam from another source and in addition to incorporate plenty of peat or leaf mould into this. Some sand is essential for the plants to get their roots into whilst the peat will help retain moisture during a dry period. This prepared soil should be made ready in plenty of time and may be placed in a heap protected from the weather by corrugated sheets or a garden light so that when required it will be friable whatever the weather may be.

To build up the rockery to the required height, stone and broken brick and other similar materials may be used and of course the soil on the site, and it is much better to raise the contour of the ground rather than to have the individual stones with too great an area showing above the ground, the appearance being quite overpowering.

The question of manure is all-important when making up the 'pocket' compost. Rank manure should not be used as this will only encourage excessive leaf growth to the detriment of flowers. Also, the plants will be 'soft' and prone to disease and pest attacks. Where it can be obtained, spent mushroom compost is ideal and I am very partial to composted straw. This should be prepared well in advance by rotting down straw or chaff with an activator. To help thorough composting, dried poultry manure may be incorporated into the straw compost. Mixed thoroughly into the loam, this will prove an excellent source of humus and food. It will also be of such a nature as to encourage ample drainage which cannot be overdone as far as the rock garden is concerned. Apart from a 1 oz. dressing of bone meal per bucketful of loam, no other artificials will be required. 'A good nourishing diet, but no frills' is what is recommended by the American specialist Louise Wilder, and this seems to be exactly what is required by most alpine plants. To put it in a nutshell the compost should be made up of:

2 parts fibrous loam, virgin turf loam if possible.
1 part coarse sand.
1 part peat or leaf mould.
1 part well decayed manure.

21

Primula denticulata

Some plants of course crave for lime, the dianthus family, for instance, and this may be supplied in the form of limestone chips or rubble. If limestone is being used to make the rockery then little will be needed in the way of additional lime, but much will depend upon the alkalinity of the soil. Likewise, if it is required to use a preponderance of acid-loving plants then the quantity of peat in the compost should be increased so as to make up at least half by bulk of the compost. It all needs careful attention before the work commences. If the rockery is being made near to conifer trees which will have saturated the ground beneath with their fallen needles, then acid-loving plants should be planted for it may be almost impossible to bring the ground to an alkaline state. Rotted pine needles may also be obtained and mixed with peat, and placed in the 'pockets' of the rockery will grow the acid-loving plants even where other alpines are also growing happily in a neutral or alkaline soil.

Climatic conditions

One may also prepare the compost to conform to degrees of climate. I have found that in the dry eastern climate of England, more humus by way of rotted manure, peat and leaf mould will be necessary and less sand, for here it is a question of retaining the maximum amount of moisture. Not only every

22

district but every garden differs greatly and so no hard and fast rule can be set down. The soil and situation of each individual garden must be closely studied before the work commences.

The stones should be laid with care, placing them in a continuous line or fall, with the grain either horizontal or vertical matching, or with the edges of much the same shape and height being placed next to each other. When once the stones are in place, a stout iron bar and spade will be necessary for moving the largest stones into the required contour, the prepared compost is rammed well down the sides of the stones and into the pockets formed by them. This compressing of the soil is of the utmost importance to conserve moisture and to prevent the formation of any air pockets into which the roots might strike and so die back when they were thought to have become well established. The surface of the stones should be tilted slightly, and so should the surface of the soil pockets, for this will allow any excess moisture to drain off during an excessively wet period. It is better to fill each soil pocket as it is made and these will of course be of various sizes.

Do not skimp the work, for this is the most important part of rock garden construction. Not only is the elimination of all air pockets of the utmost necessity, but the depth of the soil is also important. A shallow soil, which will rapidly dry out

Setting the stones

Tulipa tarda

during a dry period, must be guarded against, especially if the soil is of a sandy nature and the rockery is being constructed in a dry area. It is amazing just how far many plants send down their roots, some of them several feet, and they love to suckle up to the cool rock beneath the soil. If a stone is carefully removed after the rock garden has been established several years, the thread-like roots of the plants will be seen to have lined the sides of the cavities left by the stone. I have on occasions, when lifting and dividing members of the primula family, noticed that the strong, white roots have penetrated to a depth of nearly two feet. A deep, compressed soil is essential, but a wet, sticky soil cannot be compressed without it panning and cracking when dry and so forming air spaces which should be avoided at all costs. It is therefore better to delay this work until there is a period of fine weather or at least until the compost soil is quite friable.

As most rock plants are sold from small pots and so can be moved at any time, the best time to construct a rockery would seem to be between July and October, which will allow the plants to become established before the winter. At this period too, the weather is generally moist without being constantly wet, but even so it will be advisable to cover the filling compost, for this must not be used if at all too wet or sticky.

As the stones are placed with their surface at a slight slope, so slope the larger soil pockets for the water to drain away; especially is this necessary if the rockery is being made on level ground. Ram the compost tightly around the stones, then top up with several inches of compost into which the plants are to be set. As the work proceeds, take care to keep the stone as level as possible without any too obvious high stones, and see that both stones and soil pockets are at the same angle. The result will be a rockery of great natural beauty even before the plants have flowered.

Scree conditions

If it is required to form a scree over the whole of the rockery, a quantity of washed limestone chips or some similar material should be at hand and each pocket should be covered with an inch of stone as the work proceeds. This may be topped up after planting so as to leave it tidy. Scree-loving plants will appreciate a larger amount of peat or leaf mould in the compost and this should be made up accordingly. It is all a matter of giving the project, however small, constant thought from the very beginning. If it is desired to form a scree garden then make up the compost and choose suitable plants before the first stone is laid. Then as the work continues, do the job thoroughly, ramming the soil well round the stones, for remember that few alterations can be done when once the plants are growing and it is far better to make each stone and each soil pocket exactly as it should be before going on to the next stone.

It is now so easy to install an efficient electric pump in the garden where power is available, that the water rockery is well within the reach of the amateur. A bank or slope is necessary and of course a supply of water which may be taken from the main supply or from a natural source, by way of a well, stream or pond. By means of an electric pump the water is circulated round the rockery and so little water is needed to maintain a constant flow. By far the best stone to use for water-garden construction is water-washed limestone, which will have for centuries been washed in its natural environment in the same way as is now intended for the garden. It will be necessary to cut out of the bank sufficient soil to accommodate the large stones, which should be placed in position commencing at the bottom and building up in the same way as one would construct a house. Where it can be found, a gentle slope is far more pleasing than a steep gradient and it would be advisable to remove some of the soil from the peak to the lowest portion of the ground before the construction commences. The actual building will take the form as described when constructing an ordinary rockery, the stones sloping at the same angle, though of course they will be placed above each other rather than in a continuous line. Remember to allow a space down which the water will trickle, this will be over the stones, to the centre of the rockery, but a moraine should first have been cut away. The stones down this section must be set in concrete for soil

The water rockery

25

would be washed away by the falling water. The utmost care must be taken to make the moraine as natural as possible. Let the water work its way from one side to the other, gently falling from the stones. Let the fall be gradual and as natural as possible, and it is as well to take out a rough water course before any work actually commences. Such a rockery is always a source of delight for there is always continuous movement in addition to the beauty of stone and plant life.

Rock garden in Valley Gardens, Harrogate

4   Setting out the Plants

True alpine plants – Using good plants – The use of trees
on the rockery – Planting – The scree garden.

I feel that only true alpine plants should be grown on the scree
garden or rockery; those plants found under similar conditions
in their natural surroundings. Herbaceous and bedding plants
should be confined to other parts of the garden, where true
alpines will likewise appear equally out of place. A true alpine
plant is one that will flourish above the line of trees, possibly
somewhere between 4–5,000 feet above sea-level. Below, come
the sub-alpine plants and right down to the primulas of bogs

and marshes which are to be found at the foot of most mountains. This I have tried to carry out with my water rockery, placing the true alpines at the top, certain primulas and members of the dianthus family. Then lower down come the aubrietia and saxifrages which should have a little shade from strong summer sunshine which is provided by using miniature evergreens. Lower, come the Juliae primroses and miniature violas and ranunculus which enjoy some spray from the falling water. Then at the foot, almost with their roots in the water, are the bog primulas of Kashmir and China. In these positions, they obtain much the same degree of dryness and moisture which they do in their native surroundings, and they remain happy and healthy with the minimum of attention which is what is required of the rockery. But before any planting is done, allow the newly constructed rockery time to settle down. Let the soil settle round the stones then ram it down again, for if considerable brick or crushed stone has been used for drainage there is bound to be a certain amount of shrinkage and that means air pockets.

The selection of plants to be used should have been made even before the rockery was constructed, as the actual construction will have been made to conform to the requirements of the plants. Plants there are for the scree, like the gentians and dianthus; plants for shady positions like Kabschia saxifrages and Juliae primroses. There is a wide selection for a cold northerly situation, the ramondia and the mimulus, possibly the most colourful of all alpine plants. There are plants for an acid soil like the azaleas and the fringed orchis, the habenaria, and a wide variety of lime lovers like the dianthus and the campanulas. There are plants for a baked sunny position like the potentillas, the aubrietias and the rock roses, and do not forget the alpines with scent, such as the easily grown and deliciously almost scented Onosma, and the strongly musk-scented Muscari moschatum. It may be possible to work several of all these plants into one's rockery, but I feel that one should consider carefully the soil and situation before making a final choice. The best rockeries I have seen did concentrate on a selection of plants most suited to site and soil. For instance, if the rockery is situated in the North or where it has been given a northerly aspect and where the soil tends to be alkaline, then it will pay to plant those species suited to both the soil and aspect. Luckily, there is a wide range to cover every rock garden, and the likes and dislikes of every individual plant should be studied before planting commences.

A good selection of plants may be obtained at sixpence each, not the most choice varieties, but those that can be expected to lay a foundation for a rock garden; but I do suggest that it is better to purchase plants which have been grown in $2\frac{1}{2}"$ pots and which have formed a strong root system. The cost of carriage is far higher, a hundred plants will have to be transported by rail in a crate, whereas a hundred rooted cuttings may arrive in a small paper parcel. I have never forgotten my first plants. I was just ten years of age and had saved up my Saturday pennies (there were only pennies in those days) to order through the post a dozen border carnations. For half a crown I expected to receive plants from pots and best named varieties too, and when they flowered I expected something to conform to what I thought was the meaning of the advertisement. They arrived in an ordinary envelope and produced single pale pink blooms not quite the size of a sixpence. But it taught me a lesson I have never forgotten. So do purchase from a reliable specialist who has become known through the years as a grower of top quality plants and let my early experience be a warning.

Using good plants

Plants from pots may be set out at any time of the year without fear of disturbing the roots, but I think from late July to early October to be the most suitable planting time, whilst the soil is warm and moist. The plants will get away to a good start and will be well established before the winter. The time to plant is when the soil is friable. If it is sticky, wait a few days and this again is where the plants from pots prove the best buy, for they may be watered and placed in a cool, shaded room where they will remain quite happy for several weeks if necessary.

Planting should be done with a trowel and whilst the operation may easily be performed, grouping of the plants calls for some care. All too often is a well-constructed rockery ruined by careless arranging of the plants. Not only is it necessary to

29

*Picea albertiana
conica and Saxifrage
moschata & Aubrietia*

make the grouping of the plants as natural as possible, but it is also important to spread out the flowering period over the entire year and to provide colour over the whole of the rockery. Most rock gardens seem to be devoid of colour during autumn and winter, which is when colour is most appreciated.

**The use
of trees** Winter brightness is provided by dwarf evergreens, which also act as a foil to the rockery, lending a more natural effect and covering up those bare winter patches. Here again, selection is important; for instance, the bushy dwarf Balsam Fir, which rarely exceeds 3″ in height is happiest only in a damp soil and the cool conditions of the North, whereas the dainty little white spruce, *Picea alba albertiana conica*, enjoys a sandy soil and sunshine. From the species described in Chapter 16, make a selection and plant them about the rockery before making a start with the alpine plants. The same may be done with dwarf deciduous trees, many of which will provide autumn colour with their foliage. The taller growing trees, those which should reach a height of from 12″ or more, and those with a weeping habit, should be planted close to the stones to act as a camouflage. The beautiful little golden cypress is most attractive when weeping over a stone. Plant close to it one of the dwarf
30 cotoneasters, for the contrast of its rich red berries during

winter is superb. The careful grouping of evergreens will be the foundations against which the alpine plants will be set out. Many of these dwarf evergreens, though making little growth above the ground, send out their roots deep down into the soil, hence the need for deep soil pockets and a well-drained sub-soil into which the roots will penetrate.

When setting out the plants make the opening plenty large **Planting** enough to take the whole of the roots without trying to bend them or push them in against their will. When comfortably in, fill in with compost all around the roots and press very firmly. If the weather is dry, water them well in at nightfall. It is important to remember that the pockets which are possibly shielded from heavy rain by overhanging stone should be reserved for those plants requiring winter protection from excess moisture. Likewise, those pockets sheltered from the midday sun should be used only by those plants needing a cool aspect and a moist soil, all of which must be carefully dealt with as planting progresses. If limestone rock is being used it will be found to contain a number of holes formed by continuously falling water. These are ideal for planting with those plants that enjoy protection from soil splashing. These holes should be

Zauschneria californica   31

filled with prepared compost, made quite firm, and a most charming effect is provided by the plants tumbling down the stone. Try the aubrietias in this way and saxifrage, Tumbling Waters with its arching sprays of pure whiteness or the rich purple blooms of *Phlox douglassii*, Violet Queen, which will cascade down a stone for almost 2'. A plant which will provide a superb effect when planted in an aperture is the rich sky-blue flowered *Primula hyacintha*, which grows to a height of 4" and delights in the protection of such a position. Do your planting carefully, taking time to provide each plant with its needs, and they will well reward you with their vigour and richness of colouring.

Where the pockets are large enough, plant two or three plants of one colour or variety; in other words, plant in drifts to see them in their most striking form. Odd plants dotted about the rockery here and there will never provide the brilliance of colour of which they are capable when planted together. Two aubrietias of slightly different shades of red or crimson should be planted together, then near to them by way of contrast plant several white flowered campanulas even of different forms. It is also important to plant for an all year round display. If using crocus then plant the October flowering *C. speciosus*, and the January flowering *C. korolkowi* as well as the more familiar spring flowering varieties. They are equally as inexpensive, too. And plant in groups of four about the rockery so that no part appears devoid of colour at any time of the year. For late autumn colour there is no more colourful plant than the Californian Fuchsia, *Zauschnaria californica*, which bears its orange trumpets during September and October, but it is so colourful, plant it in groups about the whole rock garden rather than just as a single plant. And plant with it *Crocus cancellatus albus*, which produces its silvery-white flowers at the same time. The rockery in autumn will then be as colourful as during summer.

Rock plants seem to love company, individual specimens in isolation rarely flourishing as will two or three plants set out in close proximity. For this reason it is essential to make the compost as rich as possible without causing rank growth. Rank or untidy growers, or plants which are capable of seeding themselves prodigiously, should be kept away from a rock garden, for eventually they will stifle any plants in close proximity, whilst those that seed themselves in great abundance will produce such an amount of seedlings as to be almost impossible to eradicate. There are plenty of plants with a neat refined habit and one should concentrate on these. It is also advisable to keep apart those plants with a more delicate habit, from those more robust, otherwise the one will tend to crowd out the other. Neither is it advisable to over-plant a new rockery. Remember that young plants will quickly make considerable growth and if planted too closely will, in eighteen months, form a dense mat of plant growth which will tend to make the rockery a sorry sight unless kept cut back systematically. In this respect the happy medium is required, and a little soil and stone is a good thing to see amidst a mass of flowering plants.

Where the plants are being set in the scree garden, the chippings are placed over the soil and around the plants as soon as they have been planted. Or it may be that the scree has been made first and will only require a light covering of chippings round the plants to leave it tidy. Do not forget to place beside each plant a tiny wooden label with the name neatly written in Indian ink which will not fade. Correct and lasting naming is necessary to obtain the greatest interest from a rock garden. Do not neglect those plants native to one's district. There are many charming plants which grow wild amongst the rocks of Britain and it is these which should be the foundation of one's rockery. There is that dainty little dianthus, found growing amongst the rocks of Cheddar and called the Cheddar Pink; there is *Dianthus arenarius*, with its tiny white fringed blooms to be found in sandstone regions. The dainty harebell, too, looks more attractive than ever when planted against weathered Westmorland stone. In its native haunt, which is around the limestone regions of Ingleborough, the bird's-eye primrose, *Primula farinosa*, is to be found, often in abundance. The heathers may also be found naturally in many parts of Britain and are most attractive when planted in the woodland rockery along with various primulas and azaleas and bulbs which flourish under shady conditions.

The scree garden

33

It is great fun to roam the countryside in search of these native flowers, and to introduce them to one's rockery will be to enjoy a breath of one's native land even under town conditions of soot and smoke. So do not crowd out the rockery; rather should some room be left for one's native alpines and for some of those rare plants one may come across in the years ahead.

Veronica Whittleyi
& Potentilla
eriocarpa

Gypsophila repens
rosea

Rock garden pool at Wisley

5 The Propagation of Alpines

Alpines from seed – Sowing the seed – Preparing the compost – Transplanting – Division of the roots – Layering – Rooting from cuttings – Rooting compost.

To be able to increase one's own plants with a view to replacing those which become straggling or may eventually die back will add interest to one's gardening. Or on some occasion it may be decided to build another rockery or to make additions to the original one, or if the venture is a success and rock gardening gets into one's blood, it may become a profitable hobby and so a detailed knowledge of propagation will prove of considerable help. There are a number of ways by which the stock can be increased:

    (*a*) By sowing seed.
    (*b*) By division of the roots.
    (*c*) From cuttings.
    (*d*) By layering the shoots.

Alpines from seed

This is the quickest way of building up a stock of plants and a rock garden may quite easily be planted entirely with plants raised in this way. But as most choice rock plants are hybrids, there is no guarantee they will in any way resemble their parents when raised from seed. For instance, there are excellent strains of aubrietia which will give a wide range of delightful shades ranging from deep purple to crimson. However, there is no guarantee that one will obtain something resembling one's favourite variety. You may obtain purples and crimsons, but it would be surprising if one obtained a plant of a double variety or even of that lovely large steel-blue flowered variety, Studland. It is, however, great fun trying to obtain a plant with some startling characteristic or colour, a plant that one day may become a commercial variety. This is only possible if the very best seed is obtained. It will cost a little more than that saved from less meritorious plants, but it will take only the same length of time to germinate and will have been no more trouble to raise and rear. Some plants will give a far wider range of colours than others and be much easier to raise from seed; these include pansies, aubrietia, double daisies, primulas and pinks. Most alpine plants will set seed, which is generally minute in size and so must be saved and sown with care.

The seed pods should be carefully removed before fully ripened for they may then shed the seed and much would be lost. The pods should be placed on sheets of white paper and placed in a dry room where they finish off ripening and drying.

It must be remembered that alpine plants shed their seed when ripe and this frequently becomes frozen for several months before it germinates. I have found that seed sown in shallow boxes of compost and allowed to remain in the open during the latter part of the winter will germinate more readily in springtime than if the seed is sown in heat or in a cold frame in spring. Alpine seed will germinate more readily under glass where mositure conditions may be controlled and either sheets of glass may be placed over the boxes or a cold frame may be used. If propagating large quantities of plants, then a cold frame will be indispensable and where there is available room for a frame it will repay its cost over and over again. As a substitute for snow and frost, subjecting the seed to refrigeration conditions for two hours before sowing will hasten germination, but the seed should first be moistened before being frozen, otherwise damage may be done. As the seed of certain alpine plants may take some considerable time to germinate, the seed should be sown in as fresh a condition as possible. More failures in raising from seed occur through the use of old seed which has lost vigour, than through any other cause. My own method is to sow the seed in a prepared compost on or about February 1st. It is then placed in cold frames where it becomes frosted, the compost often becoming frozen right through. Leave the lights off the frames until early March so that some snow can reach the seed. Give them as near to the conditions enjoyed in their native lands as possible. Then mid-March, the frames are closed, or if a slightly heated alpine house is available then lift the boxes in, or merely cover them outdoors with a sheet of clean glass. They will have received plenty of moisture and will require almost no more attention until they germinate.

Sowing the seed

But first let us prepare a suitable seed sowing compost. The essential ingredients must be sand, peat and loam and knowing the great liking of most alpine plants for some humus and some grit to get their roots into, if equal quantities of bulk are made up the compost will be as near to their liking as possible. Or if you wish, make up the standard John Innes sowing compost or it may be obtained already made up as follows:

Preparing the compost

37

$$\left.\begin{array}{l}\text{2 parts loam}\\\text{1 part peat}\\\text{1 part sand}\end{array}\right\}\text{per bushel}$$

1½ oz. per bushel superphosphate
1 oz. per bushel ground limestone

Quite shallow boxes may be used, or seed pans, and until required, the compost should be kept away from excess rain. As the seed of certain varieties may take some time to germinate, use soil for your compost which has either been sterilized or has been dug from virgin pasture and so will be free from weed seeds which may easily choke the tiny alpines as they germinate. Alpine seed is generally so small that it is better mixed with dry sand before sowing and it should be left uncovered. Just press it into the compost when sown and if a quick germinating variety, sprinkle over a little sand. Seed may be sown at almost any time of the year. It will germinate quickly if sown in mid-summer, but otherwise I prefer to wait until February and sow as described.

Whether the seed germinates quickly or not, do not be in too great a hurry to discard the container. Certain varieties will take almost a full year to germinate. Some seed of others may germinate quickly, whilst others come along only after those that were first to germinate have been transplanted, and so all seed boxes or pans should be left a full twelve months before finally discarding, and the slow-moving varieties should be left even longer.

Transplanting

The tiny plants should first be transplanted into deeper boxes containing much the same compost, possibly a little more soil and a little less sand, and when large enough they should be moved to individual thumb size or 2½″ pots of earthenware, or compressed paper. Here the compost should be the John Innes Potting Compost made up of:

½ bushel loam (fibrous)
¼ bushel peat
⅙ bushel silver sand
1 / 48th John Innes Base
¾ oz. ground limestone

Phlox subulata

John Innes Base is made up of:

> 2 parts horn meal
> 2 parts superphosphate
> 1 part sulphate of potash

From the time the plants are ready to be pricked out into boxes or pots, care should be taken to see that they are kept growing on and too much water should not be given or the seedlings may damp off. Likewise when in the pots and in the frames, though there can be no hard and fast rule. If the weather is warm and sunny then more water should be given than say between November and March when soil evaporation is but slow. When the plants have nicely formed in the pots and before they have become pot-bound, they should be planted in the rockery, but not all will turn out as well as expected and these should be removed when they have flowered and may have proved themselves to be of poor quality. Throughout the life of the plant, from the time the seed is sown, the utmost cleanliness of utensils must be observed, otherwise a weakly, disease-troubled plant may be the result and your best plants may be lost.

Division of the roots

This is the easiest and most satisfactory method of reproduction. A wide variety of plants may be increased in this way;

saxifrages, campanulas, primulas; in fact, all those that form themselves into rosettes and those that make tufted, fibrous rooting sections, which will easily divide upon lifting. It is advisable to lift and divide in alternate years, otherwise the plants will form very large clumps with the centre portions tending to die back after being smothered and deprived of food in the soil. The plants should be lifted when the weather is damp and the soil moist but friable. The rosettes or divisions should be gently 'teased' apart, so that any damage to roots will be reduced to a minimum. It will be found that some plants will form their new roots at the collar at the point where the plant is at soil level. Constant lifting and replanting combined with top dressing is necessary if the new roots are to receive moisture and nourishment. Upon lifting, any decayed portions should be discarded and any surplus plants may be transferred to a stock bed or to small pots.

As a rule it is not advisable to use a knife to carry out division of the plants, but those plants that tend to form a thick, fleshy rootstock, from the top of which are formed new shoots, should be divided by a sharp knife to ensure that each new shoot should contain a portion of the rootstock. The individual plants should be given attention as to their form and requirements throughout the year, for almost every plant will require different treatment, and only by the study of each plant will they respond to provide vigour and colour year after year. When one becomes accustomed to root division, many plants may be divided whilst remaining in the soil, surplus rosettes or portions being removed whilst that part of the plant intended to remain will be disturbed as little as possible.

Layering

Trailing plants like aubrietia and *Phlox subulata* are best increased either by cuttings or by layering. There is often some difficulty in rooting these plants from cuttings for they tend to die back if there is too much moisture in the atmosphere. Layering is most certain and also quicker in the formation of roots. Many of those shoots trailing over the stones will be better rooted as cuttings, but there is generally at least some available soil space in which to root by layering. The most vigorous and healthy of the shoots are selected and a slight cut with a razor blade is made at a joint, taking care not to sever it completely.

Carnations are layered in the same way, but owing to their thick fleshy stem present no difficulty. Aubrietia and phlox are more exacting but with practice may quite easily be done. The shoots are then held into position in the soil by means of a hairpin or piece of wire, the compost being pressed around the shoots. Rooting will be quicker if some coarse sand is placed around the cut shoot. July is the best time to do this work for then there is generally some moisture about whilst the rooting will take place before the colder weather sets in. Should the weather be hot, the layer should at no time be allowed to suffer from a dry compost. As soon as rooted, which will be noticed when the shoot begins to grow out a fresh green colour, the cutting should be severed from the parent plant and potted into a small pot and placed in a frame. Or it may be left in its original position until the following March, then transplanted to another part of the rockery.

Professional growers use this method to root alpine cuttings by the thousand with success, but here conditions are all that can be desired. With the amateur this is different, for possibly all that is available is a roughly made frame.

Rooting from cuttings

The cuttings should be removed with a heel if possible, slips as they are called, for in this way they will root more quickly and with more certainty. Shoots which grow from a main stem, like pinks and the thymes, may be taken in this way. Ordinary cuttings are removed at a joint and both forms are inserted into a compost of peat and sand in a cold frame, or are placed into a similar compost in boxes either in greenhouse or frame. If removed in early summer, the cuttings may be inserted into a similar compost in the open ground and kept moist, but in no way saturated. Too much moisture will cause the shoots to damp off before they are properly rooted. Like layers the cuttings will be found to be rooted when fresh green growth is seen.

Where only a few are required to be rooted, these will root

more quickly if inserted in the sand and peat compost around the sides of earthenware pots. They will need constant care with watering as the compost in dry weather will rapidly dry out. The pots are best watered by standing in bowls of water for half an hour each day or when necessary.

Rooting compost   I am often asked why I do not use loam in the rooting compost. This is because unless the soil is sterilized, there is risk of introducing not only weed seeds but the dreaded spores of disease, especially damping off disease. The compost of sand and peat being almost sterile, it is necessary to move the plants to a loam compost; the John Innes Potting Compost is excellent, as soon as well rooted.

Evergreens, rhododendrons and all hard-wooded plants will root more readily if the cuttings are first dipped in a hormone solution for an hour before planting in the pots or boxes. There are a number of such preparations on the market and when using, one should abide by the makers' instructions for they are powerful rooting agents and will increase root activity, in some cases several weeks in advance of untreated cuttings.

Certain plants may be increased from root cuttings, particularly the primrose section. Pieces of the succulent roots are cut into pieces about 2″ in length and inserted into a loamy compost with the top showing just above soil level. Over the surface and covering the tops of the cuttings is placed a layer of sand and peat, covering the cuttings to a depth of half an inch. These are kept moist and in a closed frame, or they will soon produce new growth if placed under a bell jar. Even a large jam jar may be used successfully, but at all times keep them moist.

Certain plants such as ramondias and lewisias are best increased by means of leaf cuttings taken early in July. The leaves must be removed bearing a piece of stalk and these are pressed into the sand and peat compost and placed into a closed frame, where, if kept moist, they will soon root and should then be potted in the same way as for ordinary cuttings.

6   The Cold Frame and Alpine House

Frame construction – The alpine house – Suitable plants – Sterilizing the soil.

To build a rockery is only going half-way in this most interesting hobby. To maintain it and to propagate plants will add greatly to your hobby. A small alpine house will complete things and provide you with an all year round interest. Most important is the frame which will be in permanent occupation and so should be as well constructed as possible. A position of full sun is not necessary, but full shade will be against the raising of a sturdy plant. If there is only an open situation, then to shield the plants from strong sunshine let the frame face towards the north. It may be constructed of concrete, bricks or of wood. My own is made of 8″ boarding raised on a row of bricks, the back being raised on a double row of bricks to give it the necessary slant for the rain and snow to drain away. The boarding is held in position by stout stakes driven into the ground on both sides of the boarding, thus can the frame be easily moved if necessary. Covering may either be of glass or Windolite. I prefer glass on account of its weight, for a Windolite frame may cave in with a weight of snow and unless well secured with stones or ropes may be blown off during windy weather. But if glass is used have your frame light, no larger than 4′ × 4′. I made my first frame 6′ × 4′ and have regretted it ever since, for it was (and still is) far too heavy to move comfortably and much too heavy for a woman to manoeuvre. Either use red cedar wood which is very durable, or if using soft wood, keep it well painted. If the frame wood is raised on bricks this will keep it from destructive soil moulds. Most important is to keep the glass scrupulously clean and it should be cleaned with soap and hot water every June when the frame may be almost empty. Concrete blocks may be used for the frame and may either be cemented together or merely placed together. Concrete is colder, but is more durable.

43

A cold frame should be constructed over a well-drained bed. For this, remove 6″ of soil and make a bed of crushed brick or stone. Broken pot or any similar material may be used. Make it quite firm to a depth of 4″, then add a mixture of peat and sand to a depth of several inches. Into this preparation, made quite firm, the cuttings are inserted and the pots of growing plants are stood in this compost which is always kept comfortably moist. It is preferable to construct two frames or one of two lights divided into two compartments, for it is often necessary to retain a close, humid atmosphere for one where rooting is taking place, whilst growing plants will need plenty of ventilation in the other. A double-light frame will be of a size large enough to maintain quite a large rock garden at the maximum of efficiency.

The alpine house   Where there is room to erect a cold house, however small, this will prove an added asset to one's hobby and prove well worthy of the small expense required for its construction. My own is 8′ × 6′ wide and contains a well-constructed staging and shelves 4′ above. The roof has been constructed of clear glass containing three 2′ wide ventilators on either side. The glass roof provides rigidity and is not troubled by snow, but the sides are constructed entirely of Windolite which has proved completely adequate since the glass was blown out during the war and it has not been thought necessary to replace it.

The alpine house should be away from any overhanging trees which will tend to draw the plants. Should the sun prove too severe during mid-summer, when there will be little in the house, the glass may be shaded with lime-wash. It is during the coldest months that the alpine house is most in use. It may be used to house pans or boxes of cuttings which are rooting, or young plants which have only just been transferred to the pots. Again, it can be used to winter certain tender plants that may be killed by excessively wet conditions. But I find its greatest use is for those pans of dainty choice alpines which will bloom better given some winter protection, and a number of plants which will bloom earlier than in the open and so a more extensive flowering period can be enjoyed.

44

The most important part of the alpine house is the staging. We are not growing orchids or perpetual carnations and so the outer construction may be adequate but in no way pretentious. The staging should, however, be strongly constructed for having to take a good depth of shingle and sand in which to plunge the pots and pans, and together with the potted plants the load will be heavy. Stout timber should be used, with flat galvanized iron sheeting to hold the shingle bed. To ensure adequate drainage the sheeting must be drilled with numerous holes. Shingle is then placed over the sheeting to a depth of 2″, again to ensure ample drainage, and over this a 2″ depth of sand mixed with a quantity of peat will act as an ideal plunge bed. If the sand and peat is always kept moist the pans and pots will obtain sufficient moisture without additional direct watering and any risk of the plants damping off will be reduced to a minimum.

In the alpine house, under the staging, should always be available a heap of potting compost made to the John Innes formula. Here the compost will be safe from frost and snow and excess moisture and will be available whenever required.

The space underneath the staging will be valuable for rooting the small bulbs which should be used liberally for winter and early spring flowering. To ensure complete darkness, sacking or canvas should be fastened round the staging. A second plunge bed should be made here, exactly as described for the staging and into this the pans and pots of the bulbs may be placed, the shingle beneath ensuring perfect drainage. If the bulbs are planted during October they should be taken from beneath the staging towards the year end. They will come into bloom a month before those planted on the rockery.

There are also quite a number of plants that will spend much of their life in the partial shade beneath the staging. That attractive rich blue flowering ramondia is one and it will bloom under the staging towards the end of April.

To enhance the appearance of pots of alpines growing indoors, these should be covered with small shingle which will also prevent the soil splashing on to the blooms and foilage.

Plants for the alpine house

Ideal plants for the alpine house are *Primula winteri* and

Sempervivums

allionii and those delightful miniature auriculas, the pubescens group; the winter flowering hardy cyclamen; several of the gentians; the lewisias; and most of the campanulas. Most of the saxifrages and sempervivums are ideal plants for the alpine house. But it must be remembered that all alpine plants are quite intolerant of warm, moist, ill-ventilated conditions. They are natives of alpine regions and these are the conditions under which they flourish, so never over-water and open the ventilators at all times, except when the weather is wet and foggy. Those plants which cannot be planted beneath an overhanging stone, which will provide protection from the winter rains, should either be lifted and planted in pots in the alpine house at the end of October or they should be covered with a sheet of clean glass or with a cloche.

Cloches are most valuable placed about the rockery to cover tender or moisture-hating plants between November and early March and they may then be used to cover annuals or straw-berries or rows of early peas, thus more than earning their cost. During summer, cuttings may be taken and inserted in shallow trenches of peat and sand under these same cloches. Remember too, that the utmost cleanliness of all utensils, whether of cloches or pans and pots, is essential to the rearing of a sturdy, healthy alpine plant. They are never happy under dirty conditions.

46 A word should be said here about the compost ingredients.

First, the loam. This should be sterilized if possible; if not, it should have been taken from pasture land. Old, much used garden soil, often of an acid nature and containing seeds of weeds and spores of disease, must be avoided. The ideal soil for potting is a fibrous loam obtained from turf that has been stacked and has become well rotted. This should be rubbed through a sieve and mixed with sand and peat. Any coarse sand will be suitable, from river bed or seashore, but use only a good quality peat otherwise it may have a too high acid content.

It will be found of the greatest value to sterilize your soil, especially if living in a town and access cannot be obtained to turf loam. This is not a difficult operation when only fairly small quantities are required. A simple method is to obtain an extra galvanized iron sheet other than required for the staging. This is also drilled as described. A brick container for a fire is first made and the sheet is placed over the brick sides and bolstered beneath with additional bricks. Around and above the sheet are built four courses of brick and into this compartment is placed the soil. The fire is made beneath, the heat and steam penetrating through the sheet and the drilled holes to the soil. Sterilization will take place if the temperature reaches

Sterilizing the soil

Juniperus communis depressa aurea, saxifrage etc

Picea abies nidiformis

175° F. (80° C.) and remains fairly constant for two hours. Take care to see that the temperature does not exceed 210° F. (99° C.) otherwise the soil will be reduced to an inert mass and be useless. To obtain an even distribution of heat it is advisable to turn the soil with a spade every half-hour so that the bottom layer does not get over-sterilized and the top-soil left without proper sterilization.

The sterilized soil may be used when cool, when it will be ready to make up the compost.

7 Alpines for the Trough Garden and Window Box

Making a trough garden – Suitable plants – The window box rockery – Alpines in a dry wall.

One does not necessarily have to construct a rockery to enjoy plants of alpine origin. They are such accommodating little chaps that if their cultural requirements are considered, they will grow well almost anywhere, but because of their dainty compact habit they are ideal subjects for planting in stone troughs, or in a window box or in a dry wall. For trailing over a terrace wall there are no lovelier plants than aubrietias, the trailing phlox, campanulas and saxifrages. They will provide masses of bloom when the plants have been established twelve months. They require no special cultural treatment apart from planting in a loamy soil containing some humus. Plants in the confined space of a trough or window box will require more detailed treatment, but so delightful will be the result that some effort will be well worth while.

A stone trough is the ideal for the plants and the rocks used will blend in with the stone of the trough. I have, however, made use of an old earthenware kitchen sink, sunk into the soil beneath a window and the effect has proved of the utmost charm. It is advisable to chip away some of the glazed interior. Drainage will be by way of the plug hole and a similar hole must be cut into the bottom of a stone trough to allow for drainage. Two holes, one at both ends, will prove better than just one. A trough of any depth greater than six inches will be suitable, but between 10″ and 12″ will prove ideal and will allow space for correct drainage materials.

Pieces of wire netting should be squashed into balls and pressed into the drainage holes to prevent the drainage materials from falling out. A 2″ layer of crushed brick or shingle is then

Making a trough garden

placed over the bottom of the trough, and window box requirements are exactly the same, and over this an inch layer of coarse
sand. Then fix in one or two stones, deep stones which will show
only about 3″ or 4″ above the edge of the trough but which,
like on the rockery, will extend to a considerable depth beneath
the soil. Preferably let this rest on the sand then fill up the rest
of the trough with prepared compost. The best stone to use is
porous limestone, around and into which the roots of the
plants may penetrate, for it must be remembered that a confined
garden will frequently lack moisture however carefully the
watering is attended to. Sandstone and Cotswold stone will
appear most attractive, but to allow the plants a larger surface
of stone beneath the soil which will keep moist, a few more stones
should be used even if of smaller size.

The compost should consist of decayed turf loam, fibrous if
possible, into which is incorporated some peat and some sand;
also if possible a little fine shingle such as found on the seashore.
Peat I prefer to leaf mould, for it is sterile and contains no
spores of disease with which leaf mould is frequently troubled.
The maximum amount of drainage is necessary when growing
in troughs or window boxes and the compost must contain
plenty of sand. Some pieces of charcoal, obtained from the
chemist, will help to keep the compost sweet over a considerable
period. Every four or five years it is advisable to remove the
plants with care and to clean out the trough and remake it. If
the work is done in late autumn, it will have time to settle down
for the spring when it will be found to have lost little of its glory.

The compost should be filled to within a half-inch of the
top of the trough so that the soil will not be splashed over by
rain or when watering.

Suitable plants Exactly like the garden rockery, the foundation of a miniature
garden will be its tiny trees. Use several of the dwarf evergreens
and keep them trimmed, for they must not be allowed to out-
grow the other plants in size, or the effect will be spoilt. One
suitable tree is the Golden Cypress with its rich golden-bronze
foliage and its tiny deep green companion, the *Hinoki Cypress*,
Chamaecyparis obtusa, both of which are very slow growing.
The dwarf Norway Spruce, *Picea excelsa compacta nana*, is a

50

Crocus chrysanthus.
E. A. Bowles

Chionodoxa lucillae

Alyssum saxatile

Helianthemums

slow-growing little tree with horizontal spreading branches. The species *Picea maxwellii*, almost of cushion form, is also most charming in the miniature garden. For a cold northerly situation, *Pinus montana uncinata*, the mountain pine, whose foliage turns a rich golden-bronze colour during autumn and winter, and the dwarf small-leaved ivy, *hedera minima*, which will lift itself up the stones and remain evergreen through 51 winter, are plants of charm. Another lovely little ivy, *H. conglomerata*, will trail itself along the edges of the trough.

For a position which faces south and may tend to become baked in the summer sun, plant several of the dwarf brooms, the Genistas. *G. decumbens* grows no taller than 3″ and *G. januensis* only about 6″ tall and both cover themselves in tiny yellow pea-like flowers. For the larger trough garden, the new variety, Peter Pan, which makes a compact plant 12″ in height, bears showy, bronzy-crimson flowers.

Several of the heaths, too, make an attractive foundation. They like, with the exception of the carnea varieties, a compost containing plenty of peat. One of the most charming heathers is *Erica vulgaris*, Mrs. Pat, which rarely exceeds 2″ in height and whose foliage is of the most variegated colours. The variety J. H. Hamilton bears double salmon-pink flowers 6″ in height. For winter colour, *Erica carnea*, W. T. Rackliffe, white flowered, is a charming plant.

The miniature roses are ideal plants for the trough garden or the window box. They remain in bloom throughout summer and never become untidy. The smallest of them all is the pink-flowered Rouletti. Slightly taller is the new Maid Marion, which bears its rich-crimson button-like flowers in great profusion.

Do not neglect colour all the year round, even in the miniature garden. Besides the winter heathers, there is a range of charming bulbs ranging from the November flowering *Crocus longiflorus*, with its rich lavender trumpets, to the early March flowering *C. chrysanthus*, with the golden E. A. Bowles and the pure white Snow Bunting. Then there is the dainty winter aconite, *Eranthis hyemalis*, with its bright orange-cupped blooms borne amidst frilled green ruffs, which comes into bloom during the early New Year. To follow are the charming little Chionodoxas, *C. luciliae*, with its bright blue sprays 4″ tall. The saxifrage is one of the best of all plants for a miniature garden and none is lovelier or more suitable than the February flowering *S. apiculata*, which forms tight cushions of pointed leaves and tiny sprays of pale yellow flowers. To follow is the variety Aubrey Pritchard, with its attractive grey foilage and large deep rose-coloured flowers. There is a wide range of saxifrages to extend the flowering season right into autumn.

Another dainty plant is the *Douglassii*, which forms mats of shining green foliage. The species *D. laevitaga*, bears its rosy-red flowers late in summer and *D. vitaliana*, bears its pure yellow blooms in early spring. The aubrietias may be planted round the trough, especially if it is a raised trough. Compact forms of the dianthus may also be used in the miniature garden: the Cheddar Pink, *D. caesius*, with its grey foliage and fragrant rose-pink flowers; and some of those charming hybrids of which the double crimson-flowered Mars and the double salmon-pink Jupiter are neat of habit and most free flowering. Probably the tiniest of all alpines and eminently suitable for a trough garden is *Dianthus microlapis*. It likes some lime and bears its tiny clear pink blooms which rest on the foliage barely an inch in height.

Plants with trailing habit should not be used in the trough garden unless it be to cover the sides, nor should plants with too vigorous root run be used, for in the miniature garden a wide range of plants must be used in only a restricted space. Most of the plants I have suggested will appreciate and look more attractive if shingle is placed round them to prevent soil splashing and to enhance the rich colouring of both foliage and bloom. The choice of plants will be given the same consideration as when forming the rockery, aspect of trough and window box being most important.

Apart from regular watering during summer, the miniature garden will require little attention other than to cut back any straggling growth. Few weeds should appear, as the mat-like growth and shingle will stifle them. Each autumn the shingle should be removed and the compost gently forked over. It should be top-dressed with peat and the shingle replaced. It will require no other attention for twelve months.

The window box will require much the same treatment as the trough garden. The container may be either of concrete or wood containing drainage holes and it should be securely fastened to the sill. It should be prepared in the same way, but only the very neatest of plants should be used. Additional colour may be obtained by planting as many small bulbs as possible and these will push up through the foliage of the alpines.

The window box rockery

Nothing gives greater interest and charm in the garden than the dry wall, especially if it is built of either Cotswold stone or of red sandstone, both of which are extremely colourful. The wall may be used to divide a kitchen garden from the pleasure garden or it may be used to surround a sunken lawn or flower garden, or merely to hide an unsightly bank or corner. It may be of any height, but it is generally about 3'. Often it is built with a cavity in the centre which is filled with compost as the wall is built. It is topped up with soil on completion and plants are set along the top, aubrietias and rock roses (Helianthemums).

A dry wall is constructed by stones which are placed with as long a stone as possible beneath each joint to give durability. Into these joints soil is packed and there the plants are set. Large stones will give a more durable wall. Before commencing each layer, sort out the stones into similar sizes for the particular layer, otherwise the finished wall will appear uneven and far from solid on completion even if this is not so. If large, deep stones are used, a plant may be set at almost every joint, but this will be too much if a more shallow stone is being used. The soil used to accommodate the plants should contain some humus; some well rotted manure and some peat should be mixed with the soil. There will be no need to add any sand, for a too sandy compost and one devoid of humus will tend to dry out and crack during a hot period. Once again, select the plant to suit the aspect, choosing those plants suited to a shaded wall or one facing north, and where the wall is in full sun select only those used to baked conditions like the rock roses and thymes.

For a cold or shaded aspect, plant the blue lithospermum, the saxifrages and the ramondias, and there even most of the campanulas will thrive. For a sunny wall, *Alyssum saxatile*, aubrietia, all the dianthus family, Helianthemums (rock roses), the veronicas, aethionema, and more especially the sedums and sempervivums, all of which are described in detail in the following chapters. They should be firmly planted, the compost being pressed around the plant. So that they get away to a good start it is better to use plants from pots which should be soaked in water before being planted.

54

Campanula portenshlagiana

Erodium chamaedryoides roseum

8   The Paved Garden

The woodland path – Laying a crazy paving path – The terrace garden – The alpine lawn – Plants suitable for carpeting.

Quite as charming an alpine garden may be made by the use of crazy paving stones or stone or concrete flagstones than by the construction of the more orthodox rockery. Flat Cotswold stones or flagstones either of concrete or of stone, correctly and   55 carefully laid and planted with suitable prostrate plants, which against the surface of the stones will show off their colour and habit to a far greater degree than with the soil of a rockery, however well constructed. Paving may be used, (*a*) to construct a flat terrace, (*b*) to make a path round a house or about the garden, (*c*) to make a woodland path. Each will demand a different method of construction and stone of different sizes.

The woodland path   The path leading to a woodland garden or to a garden naturalized with bulbs must be made to conform to its surroundings. Flags of stone or of concrete cut to an exact size would look out of place, so would straight-edged crazy paving stone. Suitable would be flat stone of various sizes and with edges or sides which are in no way straight. The path or steps should look as if they have been in position since the beginning of time; in fact, they should be almost unnoticeable. The construction of such a path will not be difficult for there is no necessity to fit the various pieces of stone so that the sides conform to a straight line, nor is it necessary to trouble about closing up as much soil space as possible. The woodland path may be on a slight incline so as to provide as natural a position as possible and to show off the plants which will be set out down the sides and between the stones. Take care to make the stones level with the ground. This not only produces a natural effect, but will make for easier walking and as with the rockery the amount of stone beneath the soil to enable the plants to seek out the moisture and coolness provided is more important than the amount above the soil. Planting may be done at random using those plants suitable for a shady position, and there is no need to plant only those with a low habit, as is necessary when planting a more formal path.

When laying a formal path of crazy paving this is much more exacting. It is important to bring the stone to the same level, and remember that the size and thickness of every stone will be different, calling for a certain amount of care in taking out sufficient soil to enable the stones to be laid level. Then there is the care necessary in selecting the stone not only so that the straightest sides conform to the straight sides of the path, but so that only the minimum amount of soil is left exposed. The path should be as even and as level as possible to make for easier walking whilst it is important to leave as few gaps as possible. A paving path or terrace containing too much exposed soil will always be a source of trouble as far as weeds are concerned, and will never look as effective as it should do. And to plant too many plants in order to close up the gaps will give the path an untidy appearance.

When laying a path of crazy paving, first begin by marking out the necessary length and width, then remove several inches of soil depending on (a) the depth of stone, and (b) whether it is desired to lay the stone on to a thin bed of concrete.

Laying a crazy paving path

The question of the concrete bed is all-important, for not only will it provide a firmer foundation which will prevent various stones from falling below the original level, which in time they so frequently do, but it will prevent the appearance of grass and weeds which are the curse of crazy paving. No matter how well the stone is laid, placing each stone tightly together with only the minimum of soil exposed, weeds will eventually push their way up from between the stones and will be almost impossible to clear. And there is no more irksome task in the garden than trying to clear a well-laid crazy paving path of grass and weeds. The concreting will be slightly more expensive in the first instance and will take more time to lay, but will be more than worth while. Pockets between the stones may be left free of concrete at irregular intervals, but do not overdo the plants, a few look much better than too many. The still wet concrete can be removed from the pockets after sections of the path are laid.

First select your stones before the work is to begin and if possible place them into something like order by the side of the path. Small stones may be placed into convenient heaps to be used to fill in any large gaps. A better job can be made of a terrace where either flags or crazy paving stone is being used if first a solid foundation of clinker or crushed brick or stone is made. This means taking out an extra 2"–3" of soil, but a clinker foundation will make a much better base over which to place the concrete. Even where no concrete is being used on which to lay the stones, a clinker base will prove of untold value in providing additional drainage, especially if the path is at all low lying. The soil may be used to fill up the pocket, or better still, a prepared compost.

Apart from a good spade, the only tool needed will be the important spirit level which will not only ensure a neater and more professional job, but will ensure that the stones are laid level and so make for easier walking. Obtain a builder's 'level', large enough to span across the path so that the top of the stone may be kept level with the sides of the ground. From the beginning of operations, make use of the level, right from the time the clinker base is put down, for this will ensure that the concrete will also be level and will make the final laying of the stone a much easier matter. Be sure to have the flattest surface of the stone to the top, and of course the sides should be kept as near straight as possible. A neat job can be done by laying (in cement) a row of bricks down each side of the path, placing them on their sides. The contrast in colour of brick and stone adds to the finished effect and will help to prevent the soil from falling on to the concrete as this is being placed into position, whilst it also makes the laying of the level stone much easier. Remember to set the stones as close to each other as possible, for if too much concrete is used to point the path on completion, it will spoil the effect. If the stone can be laid close, no pointing needs to be done except to fill up those pockets into which it is not required to set a plant. My own method is to do the planting as the work proceeds. First make a satisfactory base which is quite level, then lay the stone in possibly 6′ lengths, completely finishing the stretch in every way before continuing with the next 6′ or so. Pockets for plants should have the concrete removed whilst still wet and this should either be filled up with compost and the plant set, or a small stick should be inserted to show the position for planting. All other pockets may then be filled with concrete and any pointing done before moving on to another stretch.

The terrace garden

Laying a path with flagstones or with concrete flags is a much easier business, for they will be of almost the same thickness;

The Paved Garden

Aubrietia

the sides will be cut quite straight whilst there will be no rough edges. Before ordering the stones, first find out the various widths in which they can be supplied, then make your path or terrace of corresponding size, remembering that it is much easier to alter your ground measurements than to cut the stone. The stones being of the same size so that they will fit close up to each other, the need for a concrete bed is not so important, but as grass will eventually grow up through the slightest crack, concrete should be packed between each stone as it is placed into position. Be sure to make your base quite solid, either beating down the soil thoroughly or making the base of clinker or brick completely firm. This is particularly important when making a terrace surrounded either by a brick or stone wall, or by a rockery which may necessitate moving a considerable amount of soil before the base is formed. Subsiding of the soil will cause the stone to fall away and not only will the effect be spoilt but weeds will soon begin to appear through the cracks. If surrounding the terrace with a wall, be sure to allow a space of 6″–12″ from the stone to the wall top for planting with wall plants which will trail down the wall.

An alpine 'lawn' is a very delightful asset to any garden. The 'lawn' may be either of irregular, flat stone or may be

The alpine lawn

of coarse grass. If the position is not well drained, and a sunken 'lawn' is more delightful than any other way, it should be of flat stones around which suitable alpines are liberally planted. A dell in semi-shade may be made to look most attractive used in this way, especially where there is an acid, peaty soil and where weeds will not flourish. The alpine grass lawn should be given a sunny, well-drained position which should be so planted with small flowering bulbs and alpine plants as to give colour all the year round. But a dry, well-drained position is essential for it to be enjoyed to the full and I would prefer such a garden down the drier east side of Britain than to the wetter west, where in an unfavourable year it may be perpetually sodden. An alpine grass 'lawn' is made by selecting a piece of flat ground or a bank which is planted with a wide selection of bulbs, then sown with grass seed. When the seed has thoroughly germinated, the various thymes and dianthus and other carpeting plants liking these conditions may be planted. Whether used to plant an alpine lawn or about the crazy paving, be sure to select those plants which do not mind being trodden upon; many of them being aromatic they will give off their fragrance and still hold up their heads to the sun.

Plants suitable for carpeting

Here is a selection of plants suitable for carpeting and I have purposely dealt with the thymes in this chapter rather than in Chapter 13.

ACAENA. Native of New Zealand and amongst the best of carpeting plants, the acaenas are evergreen of a pale green shade. The flowers produced in late summer being of almost the same colour. *A. buchanani* is most attractive whilst *A. macrophylla* is also a beauty, bearing little crimson burrs which are covered in prickles.

AETHIONEMA. The rare species *A. kotschyanum*, bearing rich pink flowers above its deep green foilage, is almost of prostrate habit.

ANTENNARIA. Called the cat's ear and is one of the loveliest of all carpeting plants, the species *A. dioica rosea* producing tufts of silver-edged foliage with fluffy pink flowers which remains in bloom throughout summer. *A. dioica tomentosa* is equally attractive, bearing grey foliage and creamy-white flowers.

ARENARIA. Known as the sandwort and a most valuable plant for a shady, damp corner, or for planting in dry walls. The species *A. balearica* produces masses of tiny white flowers above a carpet of emerald green throughout early summer. Even lovelier is *A. caespitosa aurea*, which grows into tiny golden hummocks and looks most attractive with *A. Balearica*. Then there is *A. tomentosa*, which has silver foliage. All of them may be trodden upon with freedom.

ARMERIA. Most of us know the thrift, symbolized on our threepenny piece coin, but it is the taller *A. cephalotes* that is most common. A lovely plant for carpeting is *A. caespitosa*, of dwarf habit and bearing tight green cushions studded with pink balls. Six Hills Variety from the Six Hills Nursery, now alas no more, bears very large ball-shaped flowers.

ARTEMISIA. Enjoying a position of full sun and happy in the alpine lawn is *A. glacialis*, which bears silvery foliage, very aromatic and which is of spreading habit. The more it is trodden upon the more fragant it is.

AUBRIETIA. See Chapter 13.

CAMPANULA. There are a number suitable for paving. *C. Aucheri* producing its large violet bells in May; *C. garganica*, Blue Diamond, of similar prostrate habit following on with its deep blue star-like flowers; and *C. pulla lilacina*, producing its rosy bells above tiny green tufts, being three of the best. For a shady position, the *C. pusilla* hybrids are delightful.

DRABA. Evergreen plants and bearing their yellow or white flowers during early summer, the drabas are splendid plants for a hot, dry position. Bearing its stemless little white flowers amidst a cushion of rich green is *D. dedeana*, of almost prostrate form. Possibly lovelier is *D. polytricha*, which bears rich yellow blooms above attractive cushions of silver. This species does not like a wet climate, so in the west of Britain should be confined to a frame or alpine house.

ERINUS. One of the loveliest plants for paving or a wall is *E. Dr. Hanele*, an evergreen of prostrate habit which bears sprays of glowing carmine flowers during early summer. Equally lovely is another hybrid, Mrs. Charles Boyle, with its

61

blooms of clear pink, both being enhanced by planting with the white form *E. alpinus alba*.

GERANIUM. The species *G. pylzowianum* is a superb paving plant rapidly spreading out and covering its stems in a mass of shrimp-pink flowers from May until September. It is a much too refined plant to tread upon!

GYPSOPHILA. NANA. This tiny cushion plant studded with stemless white star-like flowers is very lovely on alpine lawn or paving, and plant near it *G. fratenis*, with its pretty pink blooms.

HEDERA. For a shady position no plants are more attractive than the ivies, especially the prostrate *H. conglomerata*, the leaves fastening themselves to the stones.

HYSSOPUS ARISTATUS. This dwarf form of the herb hyssop is a charming plant for the alpine lawn or for paving, forming neat little plants which are covered in tiny vivid blue spikes all summer.

LINARIA. These dainty little plants are most attractive when planted between paving stones and so valuable is their prolonged period of flowering. Most dwarf is *L. aequitriloba*, which bears masses of richest lavender flowers. Equally lovely is *L. alpina*, the deep violet flowers having a vivid orange spot on the lower lip, whilst the rosy-pink form, *L. alpina rosea*, is, in my opinion, one of the loveliest of all alpines.

LIPPIA REPENS. This is a most uncommon but easily grown alpine of creeping habit and bearing masses of mauve-pink flowers like those of scabious. The white form, *Alba*, is equally lovely.

LITHOSPERMUM. This is a superb plant for paving, remaining in bloom from May until early autumn and forming a mat of pale green foliage covered with star-like bloom. The hybrid Grace Ward is of intense gentian blue, whilst Heavenly Blue is of rich indigo-blue. They like a soil devoid of lime.

MENTHA REQUIENI. There is no lovelier carpeting plant, not so much for its beauty, but for the refreshing fragrance of its peppermint scented leaves, which give off the scent when trodden upon.

PAROCHETUS COMMUNIS. The vivid blue 'Shamrock Pea' of trailing habit and in bloom during winter is an interesting plant, but must be planted only where the winter climate is kind, otherwise it is better in the alpine house.

PHLOX. All the alpine phlox are suitable for crazy paving and more especially the *Douglassii* Section which are of prostrate habit, Violet Queen bearing a carpet of purple and May Queen sheets of purest white.

PRIMULAS. The best for filling up pockets of paving is the dainty *P. clarkii*, which forms a tuft of pale green which is covered in spring with masses of bloom of the richest and purest shade of pink of all garden plants. For the trough garden too, this is a charming plant. *P. minima*, of similar habit and which bears huge flowers of vivid crimson, is also suitable.

RAOULIA. These tiniest of all alpines enjoy a moist root run and as little moisture on the foliage as possible and so are happiest planted amongst crazy paving. *R. australis*, with its silver foliage and fluffy pale yellow flowers, is charming, and so is the prostrate *R. lutescens*, with its grey foliage and golden flowers produced in autumn.

SAPONARIA. Quickly forming large prostrate mats and covering themselves with a mass of bloom, the saponarias are valuable plants for crazy paving but tend to die back after becoming established and so a continuous supply of plants should be propagated from cuttings. Two outstanding species are *S. caespitosa*, which bears clusters of pale pink flowers, and *S. ocymoides rubra*, which covers itself with a mass of carmine-red flowers, early in summer.

SAXIFRAGA. There are quite a number suitable for crazy paving, particularly the cushion saxifrages, the tiny crimson flowered *Delia*, the cherry-pink *Arco-Valleyi* and the lilac *Amitie*. Grace Farwell forms neat grey cushions and flowers of salmon red, whilst His Majesty is a pure white flowering hybrid of similar habit. Rare and beautiful is *S. Prossenii*, which bears deep green cushions and flowers of unusual buff-orange.

SEDUM. These are plants with an enormous range of species and varieties, almost all of them ideal for the paving garden. We know them as Stonecrop, at their best in full sun where their various tinted foliage shows to greatest advantage. The species *S. anopelatum glaucum*, with its silvery foliage, is most attractive, whilst Coral Carpet forms rich green clumps, turning

63

bronze in autumn. *S. dasyphyllum*, prostrate, forms dainty glaucous green hummocks which turn rich mauve, whilst *S. lydium* turns from deep green to flaming scarlet. *S. hispanicum aureum* forms exquisite mats of gold and *S. oregonum* bronze rosettes with heads of orange. *S. middendorfianum* is an interesting plant bearing golden flowers followed by scarlet seed pods, whilst *S. spathulifolium* forms rosettes of mealy grey leaves and vivid golden flowers.

THYME. 'I know a bank where the wild thyme grows', wrote Shakespeare and nowhere are these charming old world plants happier than planted on a sunny bank or amidst crazy paving where they receive full sun. The foliage of all the thymes is richly aromatic, but none is more refreshing than the lemon fragrance of Lemon Curd, an almost prostrate thyme. *Thymus herba-barona*, which bears lilac flowers in June, has caraway-scented foliage, whilst *T. villosus*, which forms a mat of grey foliage, possesses the fragrance of verbena. But perhaps the most valuable of the thymes is *T. serpyllus* and its many hybrids and varieties, none of which grow more than 1″ tall, with *serpyllus minus* even more dwarf. Outstanding is *T. serpyllus coccineus*, which bears masses of rich crimson flowers, and with it plant the white counterpart, *albus*. Really lovely is the new Pink Chintz, which covers itself with flowers of a pretty shade of salmon.

9 Care of the Established Rock Garden

The need for constant attention – Trimming the plants –
Those colourless spaces – Importance of mulching – The use
of cloches – Watering.

It is always a tragedy to see what must at one time have been
a well constructed and carefully tended rockery now a tangled
mass of weeds and plants each contesting the right to find space
to breathe and take what nutriment remains in the soil. Unlike
the woodland garden which may be allowed to grow at will,
with almost all weeds blotted out by the overhanging trees and
copious amounts of leaves which form a continuous mulch,
the rock garden must needs be given constant care and attention.
A few minutes a day or at week-ends will keep it tidy and the
plants flourishing, for remember that each plant is different of
habit and requirements and only by considering each plant on
its individual merits will it respond as we would expect it to.
A few minutes spent each week looking over the entire rockery
will mean that it never becomes infested with weeds, nor alpines
in weed-like numbers caused by some of the plants seeding
themselves in too great abundance.

Annual weeds generally present little trouble; it is the deep
rooting dandelions and similar perennials which, if allowed to
grow into large plants, will rob the alpines of both food and
moisture and cause considerable root disturbance when they are
removed. If weeds are removed when only tiny plants, the work
is soon done and no damage will have been caused. Take the
greatest care when removing weeds to cause as little root disturbance to the plants as possible and see that the soil is pressed
well round the roots if even the slightest disturbance take place.
Remember that what goes on beneath the soil level is more
important than what happens above. When removing stubborn
weeds it is as well to hold the alpine plants with one hand
whilst removing the weed with the other, and so cause as little
disturbance as possible.

During winter it will be advisable to go round the rockery every week, though there may be but little colour to create interest. But both slugs and frost can cause damage. Slugs are dealt with in the following chapter, but frost is equally trouble- some, especially with newly planted plants which have not yet formed a strong rooting system, by causing them to become lifted from the soil. For this reason it is advisable to use plants from small pots with their roots well established when planting during late autumn and winter. Snow is always a blessing to the rockery for it will keep the plants warm and also provide a protection from cold, drying winds. For this reason I do like to see some snow covering a newly made rock garden.

I repeat that nothing is more unsightly than a tangled mess of plant life on the rockery, one plant growing into another so that the charm of one is lost in the other, colours being hopelessly mixed and the individual forms being difficult to distinguish, all of which nullifies just what a rockery should be like. So, as colourful as they might be, omit such rampant growers as trailing nasturtiums and Sedum spurium, and keep the naturally seeding plants, like myosotis, well under control, giving them a corner to themselves and if the rockery is small omit them altogether.

Trimming the plants

Even the trailing perennial plants will require considerable attention if they are not to become a jumbled mass of foliage, much of which will die back, look unsightly and will often cause the death of those plants it might cover. Aubrietias and phlox, as lovely as they are, both need attention in this respect immediately after they have flowered. Cut away all straggling growth, which not only helps the plant itself but which gives those still to bloom, air and space to reach maturity so allowing their blooms to be appreciated to the full. It is advisable where possible to cut back any plants not later in the season than early in August, to enable them to make new growth again before winter. A word of warning about cutting back. Use the utmost care and discretion, for any undue hacking of a plant will cause it to lose its form and so its attractiveness, whilst it may also cause it to die back if too much foliage is cut out too late in the year. I must say I like to see a little soil and some of the stone about a rockery; I like the various plants to show their individuality and this is only possible if one devotes just a little of one's spare time to weeding and trimming, which is a much better word than cutting back which may mean too severe cutting. Any dead wood such as one may see on heathers or the dwarf shrubs or conifers should be removed and any shoots which appear to be making too rapid growth should be cut back at a convenient point. In this respect much will depend upon the size of the rockery. Always bear in mind the individual needs of the plants; some resent any mutilation, others are given increasing vigour by trimming, some will respond better if this is done in spring, others in late summer. Almost every plant demands different treatment and they will only respond to the gardener who studies their likes and dislikes from the time the rockery is made and planted.

The stones, too, should be kept free of soil which is often dropped over them when any planting takes place. The rocks should be brushed clean when the work has been done.

Filling up any spaces which may be noticed in the spring or autumn where a plant may have died off, must be done if the rockery is to keep up its appearance. Spaces devoid of colour must be replanted at once. This is where the suitable annuals come in, for the seed may be sown in early summer if too late for planting many alpines and a splash of colour will be enjoyed during late summer and autumn. But growing on the rooted cuttings in small pots will ensure a supply of plants for planting out at almost any time. Indeed if the rockery is small, a continuous display of colour may be enjoyed all the year round if the small pots are planted beneath the surface, the plants being arranged as naturally as possible and these may be removed after flowering and replaced by others in bud or bloom. A small cold frame to take the pots will be a great help. Bulbs may be used in this way; those which bloom during winter may be replaced in spring by those about to bloom. This will create a little more work, but will ensure a continuous

Those colourless spaces

67

display and is a specially suitable way of keeping up the colour in the window box.

Correct naming of the plants calls for some care. The best labels to use are those made of white plastic material, the names clearly printed in Indian ink, which is unaffected by water. The labels should be pushed into the soil or pot close to the plant, so as to be unnoticed except when it is desired to refresh one's memory as to the variety. Rooting cuttings should also be carefully named in the frames, for half the fun is taken from rock gardening if the plant names are lost.

Importance of mulching

Then there is mulching, so often neglected. Not only will a mulch provide an additional winter protection, but will keep up a continual supply of humus in the soil and will stifle most annual weeds. Even more important is that a number of plants, notably various members of the primula species, form their new roots from the collar at soil level. These roots tend to push the plants out of the ground and if not mulched or lifted and replanted each year, the new roots will die back and so will the plant. A mulch of peat or of prepared compost will give the roots the necessary covering. After flowering always seems to be the best time for mulching. Remove any dead blooms and straggling growths and then press the mulch – peat, sand and loam is ideal – around the plants. It is surprising how well they respond in the formation of fresh green growth. Certain plants should be given a mulch of shingle or coarse sand early in winter. This will help to prevent excessive moisture remaining about the crowns and splashing on to the leaves, for some of the mealy-leaved plants are intolerant of excess winter moisture even if unharmed by very cold periods. Plants unduly troubled with the wet of winter are, I find, best set out in their small pots, so that they may be removed to the shelter of the cold, yet dry alpine house in early November, but much may be done by heaping fine shingle, sand or weathered ash about the crowns during November. Or they may be covered with a small sheet of glass or a cloche, if it is not possible to give them the protection of the rocks themselves. Some of the small, not quite hardy bulbs may be planted under the heathers which will afford some protection. If glass is used see that it is always kept clean.

Glass may also be judiciously used to bring various plants, including bulbs, into bloom before their natural time, but remember that you are dealing with alpine plants, used to cold regions and at all times ample supplies of air must be admitted to the plants. The use of a cloche, leaving the ends open, will help to bring the plants into bloom a little earlier than normally and protect the more tender winter flowering plants from fog and soot deposits. Cloches, too, are useful to give any newly planted alpines some protection from cold, drying spring winds until they become established. More plants are harmed by drying winds in spring when producing the new seasons growth than by any other cause. If no glass is available, then erect a wattle hurdle at the side of the rockery against the prevailing winds. This may be removed when the weather becomes more favourable. Even twigs and small branches of evergreens inserted into the soil around the more tender plants will provide much appreciated protection.

The use of cloches

It is advisable to remove all leaves from the rockery, those which may have fallen from nearby trees in late autumn and which become lodged about the stones and plants. They not only look most untidy, but will become saturated and may cause nearby plants to rot away should the winter be unduly wet. To give protection, I prefer the shingle and sand method, or small branches of evergreen may be placed over the plants.

Watering is most important, especially during spring and summer. Of recent years, lack of rain and drying winds which scorch the plants during April and May, has caused considerable damage and it is then that the hose or watering can is most needed. Correctly set stones which extend to a good distance underground will help to keep the roots cool and moist. It is during periods of drought that the well-constructed rockery pays dividends for one's labours. Likewise, if the main contour of the stone is placed against the prevailing winds, excessive

Watering

drying will be guarded against. Newly set out plants should be well watered in, but in a period of drought they will tend to dry out especially in the drier districts of the south and east. At sundown, the plants will most appreciate a soaking and a spraying of the foliage. They will be refreshed and come up smiling next morning. Even if it is not considered necessary to give water at the roots, syringing of the foliage in hot weather, given when the sun is off the plants, will prolong their flowering season and keep them clean and fresh and free of red spider.

When living in the centre of one of our industrial cities, I used to sponge the foliage of glossy-leaved plants when I had a few moments to spare. This kept them free of soot deposits and they paid ample dividends. Plants set out in pots, or those in trough gardens or window boxes will require more watering than those set out in the open ground. There is no rule of thumb, but the true alpine lover will look to the requirements of his plants every day. A heap of compost made up in the alpine house or shed and always on hand for filling around the plants, and a syringe of cold water will help to keep the individual plants clean, nourished and comfortable throughout the year.

The crazy paving garden will present few worries, for the plants will either be those requiring almost no moisture, like the thymes or those which have a creeping root run and which are able to find all the moisture they require beneath the stones. The plants should be trimmed occasionally, and they will also appreciate a mulch of peat or compost gently pressed around the plants in autumn. Any plants which appear to be short of compost in the dry wall will also be helped by pressing compost about their roots whenever necessary, and such plants will also benefit from an occasional spraying throughout the summer.

Rock and water garden

10 Pests of the Rock Garden

Aphis – Root aphis – Red spider – Slugs – Wireworm –
Caterpillars – Mildew – Rust.

As the alpine plant will be as free from disease as it is possible
to be, troubled only by occasional damping off of the crowns
during a winter of exceptional wetness which may be almost
totally averted by the correct use of the stones and by providing
scree conditions for those most liable to suffer in this way, one
need have little fear of healthy stock being attacked by disease.
Pests are another matter and constant watch must be kept for
attack. Due to the natural habit of many of the plants forming   71

dense mossy clumps, an ideal hiding place for earwigs and slugs, a constant vigil must be kept, but first remember that a sturdy plant, well grown from the beginning, will be able to combat any disease or pests to a much greater extent than a sickly, weak plant.

APHIS. In the alpine house and during a dry period outdoors this may prove a troublesome pest. By aphis is meant the white fly and greenfly which attack the succulent leaves of auriculas, sempervivums and other similar plants, sucking out the sap which not only drains the vigour from the plant, but which also makes the plant liable to virus attack, also weakening its condition. As prevention is better than cure, those with an alpine house would be advised to introduce a white fly parasite which may readily be obtained from one of the Agricultural Institutes. This will keep down the pest to a minimum. Or the plants should be systematically syringed with a suitable insecticide. I have always found Molluscide, as advocated by Mr. T. C. Mansfield in his *Alpines in Colour*, to be a safe and satisfactory preparation, safe in use and harmless to all alpines. Certainly it should be used when the pests are noticed, but better still it should be applied as a preventive measure once every fortnight. Greenfly, more readily controlled than white fly, may be brought under control by spraying the foliage with liquid derris or a solution of soft soap which should be repeated every fortnight until control is assured.

ROOT APHIS. This pest generally confines its attention to the auricula and primula race, but is liable to attack any succulent rooted plants. As with white fly and greenfly, an attacked plant shows signs of yellowing of the leaves then quickly shows loss of vitality. Complete extinction may follow. Owing to the pests surrounding themselves with a woolly mould-like substance they are difficult to kill when once they become established on the plant. This woolly aphis does not attack either leaves or the buds, but sucks the sap from the fleshy roots and is especially active during early autumn. As a cure, methylated spirit applied with a soft brush round the collar has proved effective and it may even be necessary to lift any affected plants, wash away all soil from the roots and dip them into the solution, repotting or planting into clean soil. A newer preparation, Gammexene, has proved effective when used as a dust, but a too concentrated application mixed into potting soil may harm the roots. Pestox 3 at a strength of 1 part to 200 of water and sprayed round the collar has given 100% control, but as yet it is too early to know whether the plant is in any way harmed.

RED SPIDER. This may prove troublesome to those alpines situated and enjoying dry, sunny conditions and where a continued drought is being experienced. This is a most troublesome pest, for it may infest a plant the whole year round and is generally not observed until the damage it is causing is noticed by the plant suddenly losing vigour. A very simple preventive is to give the plants some moisture. Such plants as do prefer dry conditions will naturally not take kindly to a soil provided with too much moisture, so the best thing is to give the foliage a twice weekly syringe with clean, cold water, getting the spray well under the foliage. Red Spider hates moisture in any form and may be kept at bay in the cold frame by this syringing and by keeping a constantly moist atmosphere.

Should the pest prove difficult to eradicate on plants growing outdoors, which may be so when weather conditions are excessively dry, it may be necessary to give a weak solution of a petroleum spray, following closely the makers' instructions.

SLUGS. Possibly this is the most troublesome pest of the rock garden, for the cool, moist conditions caused by the stones and beneath the foilage of plants is exactly what the slug enjoys most. One of the best preventives is to keep the rockery clean and tidy, free from weeds and straggling growth. Then during a period of rain, possibly when the plants are less vigorous than during spring, the pests will prove most troublesome, eating through the succulent growth and on many occasions killing the plant or greatly reducing its vitality by consuming the much needed leaves. It is at night when the pest is most troublesome and it is then that it should be exterminated, when most active. Much can be done by going out on a warm evening and, with the aid of a torch, picking off any slugs with a trowel and destroying them. An effective method of extermination is to use the new liquid slug preparation now to be obtained from horticultural chemists. It is poisonous only to slugs and is sprayed over the plants and   73 ground at regular intervals. Or the older method of using crushed Metaldehyde with bran and placing it in little heaps about the rockery will prove useful, but see that it is kept away from children.

WIREWORM. This pest may prove troublesome when the rockery is being made on land of a virgin nature, for it is in pasture which has been long undisturbed that wireworm proves most troublesome. Before commencing to plant up a rock garden being constructed from turf, it will be advisable to determine whether wireworm is present in any quantity and to treat the soil with naphthalene powder to exterminate the pest before the plants are set out. Half an ounce per square yard should be raked well into the soil when dry. The soil should be well forked about for at least three weeks before any planting is done, so as to release and clear it of all fumes.

CATERPILLARS. Included in this section are the soil-inhabiting caterpillars which devour the roots and which are even more troublesome than those which eat the foliage and are readily removed with the fingers. There is a safe Derris spray called Katakilla, which is also valuable in controlling red spider and which should be applied as per the makers' instructions. It is mixed with water and is quite harmless to use.

DISEASES

Few diseases will cause the alpine grower any trouble except perhaps rust and mildew, both of which will destroy the vitality of the plant, but which are readily controlled.

MILDEW. In a humid, warm summer the leaves and stems of certain plants, such as the miniature roses, may be attacked by a white mealy substance called mildew. It may be controlled by dusting plants in the alpine house or frame and even in the open with flowers of sulphur, or a liquid sulphur preparation of a proprietary make may be used where the trouble proves difficult to cure. Prevention being better than cure, it is wise to give plants a dusting with sulphur as routine and use green sulphur if obtainable, for it is not noticed on the plants.

74   RUST. This is a disease which sometimes attacks the underside

of leaves and stems of plants growing in a dry position. It may be cured by spraying the plants with Bordeaux Mixture made at home by mixing equal quantities (this may be varied) of lime and copper sulphate. Use 1 lb. of lime which is slaked with water and made into a thin paste and 1 lb. of copper sulphate. The dissolved copper sulphate is added to the lime in a wooden utensil for it is a corrosive substance, and to the whole is added ten gallons of water. It may be stored in strong glass bottles and used when necessary or as routine.

It should be remembered that both diseases and pests may be reduced to a minimum by using only strong healthy plants, giving them a soil prepared to their requirements, and by keeping the rockery clean and tidy. In addition, constant supervision of the rockery will keep any trouble at bay for measures may be taken at once to eradicate the trouble before any extensive damage is done.

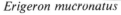

Erigeron mucronatus   *Viola odorata*

PART II

11 Plants for a Northerly Position

Most alpines are quite happy in a neutral soil and under most aspects, provided they are not extremes. There are, however, various plants which will flourish under a cold, northerly aspect, possibly one that is wind-swept and anything but kind to plant life. Most of these plants like a soil containing plenty of humus and a high degree of drainage material, for though intense cold will do them no harm, cold along with excessive moisture in the soil will cause nothing but disappointment. Plants on a sun-baked rockery will not require an undue amount of attention to drainage provided the soil is friable and excess water can drain away. Plants on a rockery where they receive only the minimum amount of sunshine must rely on ample drainage to take off excessive moisture, especially during winter. Remember that a cool, moist soil is very different to a cold, wet soil. It is the first of these conditions that the following plants will enjoy.

ANEMONE. Not only will the Dutch St. Brigid and de Caen anemones, those grown on an intensive scale for cut flower purposes, be colourful and quite happy on the rockery, but a number of the charming species will flourish on a rockery with a northern slope. They like a soil containing plenty of humus. The most outstanding species for the rockery is *A. alpina*, which bears fern-like foliage and covers itself in masses of star-shaped flowers, white shaded, pale blue and borne on 8″ stems. *Anemone vernalis* is also perfectly happy on a rockery. This is the Lady of the Snow of the Alpine regions, easily grown from seed and which bears its pearly-violet blooms on dainty 4″ stems. *A. blanda* should not be neglected on the rockery, for it is the first to bloom, early in March. It is of dainty habit, the blooms being of rich violet-blue.

ASTILBE. Most of us know the tall growing astilbes, of the herbaceous border, yet there are several tiny rock species of exquisite charm and which are quite inexpensive. They are extremely useful in that they bloom late in summer, when the rockery is beginning to look somewhat bare. A superb variety is *A. glaberrima saxosa*, which bears its stiff little spikes of feathery pink on 6" stems.

BELLIS. These are the familiar double daisies and no more charming plants are ever grown on the northerly rock garden. This plant may easily be grown from seed but will not come true to colour and habit and if those three delightful varieties, Dresden China, salmon-pink; Rob Roy, deep crimson; and, The Pearl, pure white, are required, they are increased by division. These named daisies grow only 3"–4" tall and have a neat habit and long flowering season.

CAMPANULA. So wide is the range of these hardy and easily grown alpines and so valuable are they for a cold position that they should be grown on every rockery. There are varieties that will provide colour from late in April until well into October. The first to bloom is *C. punctata*, which bears its tubular white bells on 10" stems. Then for May and June plant the lovely *C. spruneriana*, which bears its mauve and shaded bells on 8" stems. For June and July, there is *C. pilosa major*, which has dwarf shiny green leaves and large deep blue cup-shaped flowers. July and August will see *C. pulla*, G. F. Wilson, the dense mats of foliage being covered with large purple bells. Then for early autumn, plant *C. pulloides*, with its glorious purple bells.

Another lovely early autumn species is *C. lynchmere*, with its grey-green foliage, and slaty-blue flowers. Nor must the useful *carpatica* section be neglected. Superb is White Star, with its large white cups, and Chewton Joy, with its cups of rosy-lilac.

ERIGERONS. Few realize that not only is this a good border plant but several species are most attractive on a rockery and in a humus-laden soil in a cool position. They are so valuable in that they have a very long flowering season. *Erigeron alpinus*, of tufted habit and bearing rich pink flowers, blooms early May, whilst the deep orange species *E. aurantiacus* will bloom through June and July. Flowering through summer is the pale pink Elstead Rose, whilst none is more charming than the deep violet *E. radicatus*, which bears its orange-centred flowers on only 2" stems.

Anemone vernalis

Anemone blanda

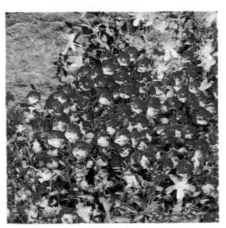

Campanula carpatica

Gentiana acaulis

Gentiana Sino-ornata

Primula nutans

GENTIANA. Most of these aristocrats of the rockery prefer a cool position and a soil containing plenty of peat. Whilst the gentians are mostly early autumn flowering, several bloom through summer, in fact *Gentiana acaulis* bears its brilliant violet-blue trumpets during early spring. Likewise *G. verna*, of prostrate habit and bearing trumpets of intense blue. *G. purdomi* bears its clusters of violet-blue flowers from early July and then come the early autumn flowering species, the most striking of all being *G. macaulayi*, Well's Variety, its large intense blue trumpets being striped with green and it is a plant of very easy culture. Almost as lovely is *G. farreri*, its Cambridge blue trumpets being shaded white inside. For late autumn, flowering right into November, is the easy and beautiful *G. sino-ornata*, which bears its Oxford blue trumpets in profusion. A newer variety flowering the same time is Kidbrooke Seedling.

MIMULUS. This is the musk flower, whose brilliantly coloured flowers should be on every rockery. If given a cool position they will remain in bloom right through summer. Almost carpet-like in its habit is *M. primuloides*, which bears masses of dainty yellow flowers, whilst almost as dwarf is the pure lemon coloured Citrona. A variety of unusual colouring is Cerise Queen, whilst H. T. Johnston bears golden tubular flowers, spotted with crimson. Similar in colouring is Merstham Hose-in-Hose like the primroses of that type, the blooms

Ramonda myconi

79

appearing one from the other. For brilliance of colouring the two outstanding varieties are Whitecroft Scarlet and Nasturtium, both of compact habit and of fiery-red colouring. This plant is increased by root division.

PENTSTEMON. I find that these attractive plants do well in a rockery protected from the midday sun. They like a well-drained ground and a soil containing plenty of grit. One of the loveliest species is *P. nitidus*, which blooms early in summer. Its vivid Cambridge blue flowers and silvery foliage make it a most attractive combination. The species *P. roezli* is of similar habit and flowering time and bears carmine-pink flowers. Another which blooms in early summer is *P. confertus*, which bears tiny spikes of creamy-yellow. Later flowering from July to September is *P. crandalli*, its dainty mauve-pink flowers appearing from feathery grey-green foliage.

PRIMULA. This is a section so vast that several large volumes have been devoted entirely to these attractive plants. Almost all of them will flourish in any position, provided some shade from the hot summer sun can be given, but the alpine types prefer a cool, northerly position and a soil containing plenty of moisture-holding humus by way of decayed manure, peat or leaf mould. They are one of the few plants of the rock garden which do enjoy some nitrogen by way of well-rotted manure.

The *pubescens* types, like tiny auriculas, are described under the chapter devoted to the Cold Frame and Alpine House. The Candelabra or Asiatic primulas are described under Chapter 14. The easiest of all the hardy primulas are the Juliae primroses and the old doubles and hose-in-hose, particularly those of primrose habit rather than of polyanthus form. About three hundred varieties are known, all of them being described in detail in *Primroses and Polyanthus* (Faber). For the rock garden one of the very best is the salmon and cherry shaded, E. R. Janes, which blooms profusely during March, April and May and again in autumn. Another with a neat, compact habit is the velvet-crimson Charles Bloom; and as a contrast Snow Cushion possesses the ideal rock garden habit. The lovely Purple Splendour is of excellent habit and so is the silvery-pink flowered Madge. A magnificent alpine primrose is the rich

80

golden-yellow hose-in-hose, Canary Bird; whilst of extremely compact habit is the hose version of the crimson-purple, Pam. And one could go on, but there are other species of equal merit.

A little known primula of such easy culture is *P. amoena*, like a tiny purple polyanthus which blooms during May. *P. forrestii* bears its umbels of sweetly-scented yellow flowers during mid-summer. *P. hirsuta* has sticky pointed leaves and bears its umbels of pinky-white blooms on 4″ stems. Also summer flowering is *P. nutans*, but as it does not enjoy excessive winter moisture, plant it in a crevice. Its powder-blue flowers are borne on 15″ stems and are of outstanding beauty. The lovely little *P. frondosa*, with its mealy-grey rosettes and heads of rosy-coloured flowers, is always at home on the northerly rockery. Having toothed petals of mauve-pink with an attractive green eye, *P. scapigera* is a charming species, but if possible let it shelter under an overhanging rock. And do not forget *P. vulgaris coerulea*, the blue flowered primrose which looks so charming planted in drifts especially where light coloured stone is being used and it is such an easy plant to raise from seed.

RAMONDA. Natives of high up in the Pyrenees, these lovely plants should be given the protection of a crevice facing due north as they must be given completely cool conditions. Given such a situation and a soil containing plenty of humus, *Ramondia myconi* is perhaps the loveliest plant of the rockery. From flat rosettes of leaves it bears its lovely golden-centred pale-blue flowers on 5″–6″ stems during early summer.

There is also a lovely white variety and one bearing rich shell-pink flowers, all equally beautiful.

SAXIFRAGE. This name comes from two latin words, *saxum* and *frangere*.

ENCRUSTED SECTION

These form rosettes and surround themselves with offsets, which as they develop, make the plants into clumps. All have branching flower stems and most like lime and sun. *S. aizoon* and the taller *S. longifolia* are examples.

While species in the encrusted section like a sunny fairly dry position, the mossy saxifrages and the kabschias or cushion varieties enjoy a moist, cool situation.

MOSSY SECTION

These dainty little plants bloom during late spring and early summer and may be planted at random throughout the rockery, but they are at their loveliest planted three together. The most dwarf, such as the crimson Pixie, bloom on 4″ stems. The tallest, the fleshy-pink flowered Holgate Gem, does not exceed 9″ in height. In between is the new large flowered crimson, Sir Douglas Haig, the icy-white Miss Britton, the rich rose-pink Cambria Jewel and the arresting crimson veined white Queen of the Belgians.

KABSCHIA SECTION

Most plants of this section come into bloom early in the New Year and continue until those of the Mossy section come into bloom in May. Only one or two exceed a height of 3″ and all are useful and possibly at their loveliest in the alpine house. One of the loveliest and first to come into flower is *S. burseriana sulphurea*, the large pale-yellow blooms being carried on sturdy red stems. There is a lovely white flowered companion called Gloria. Outstandingly lovely is *S. grisebachii Wisley*, one of the taller growing in this section, the rich crimson spikes being carried above brilliant silver rosettes. Very attractive is the hybrid L. G. Godseff, the orange buds opening to a deep yellow coloured bloom, whilst quite as lovely is Myra, which bears large cherry-salmon blooms similar in colour to Primrose E. R. Janes. A dainty variety is *S. Amitie*, which bears lilac blooms held above rich grey foliage.

SPIRAEA. These are lovely little plants, members of the same race as their tall-growing brothers which frequently reach a height of 6′, whilst the tiny rock shrublet *S. decumbens* produces its flat white heads on but 6″ stems. It blooms, as does the glorious shell-pink *S. digitata nana*, during July and August and loves a cool soil and a position protected from the hottest part of the day.

TIARELLA. This is a charming, but little known alpine plant producing feathery creamy-white spikes on 9″ stems throughout summer. The hybrid *T. wherryi* is the best, being of compact habit and so long in bloom.

Veronica cinerea

TRADESCANTIA. Loving the northern border, there is a charming little dwarf species which likes the same situation on the rockery. This is *T. brevicaule* which bears its pale crimson flowers from May to November. The flowers are most interesting in that they appear from a long leaf-like collar which greatly adds to their charm.

VERONICA. There are many charming varieties of this interesting shrubby plant, which are quite happy on the rockery either in full sun, in shade or on a northerly slope. There are veronicas to bloom from May until November and so are indispensable members of the rock garden. The first to bloom is the May flowering *V. rupestris* and its several charming varieties, the two loveliest of which are the sky-blue Silver Queen and the deep shell-pink Mrs. Halt which produce their spikes on 4″ stems. Flowering at the same time is *V. cinerea* which bears spikes of vivid blue from its silver-green foliage. Plant close to it the tiny shrublet *V. Cranleigh Gem* which with its grey foliage and silver-white flowers produces a most charming effect when planted near red sandstone. For late summer flowering, plant *V. incana* with its violet spikes and silvery foliage, and the delightful pink form, rosea.

VIOLAS. There are many lovely minute violas from which to choose. To my mind they are the best of all the race in that they are of neat habit and rarely become straggling. One of

83

the loveliest is the species *V. arenaria rosea* which is like a pure pink violet. Of similar habit is *V. gracilis major* which bears a bloom of richest purple, and the lovely white form, Clarence Elliott. But none is more arresting than the rich buff-orange-coloured Chantreyland, a plant which comes true from seed and remains colourful throughout the summer. All the small-flowered violas are suitable for the cool northerly rock garden and besides those mentioned there is the tiny flowered and sweetly scented Buttercup; the creamy-white Little David, with the fragrance of freesias; and the rich lavender-coloured Lorna. The scented violettas raised by the late D. B. Crane are also suitable.

12 Plants with a Liking for Chalk

Whilst most plants, with the exception of those which prefer conditions of acidity, will be quite happy when growing in a soil with a distinct lime content, a number prefer and will flourish in a soil containing a heavy chalk content and these should form the basis of a rockery being constructed in a garden with a chalk-laden soil.

AETHIONEMA. This is one of the loveliest of all chalk-liking plants. It likes a sunny, dry soil where it will thrive even where chalk is lacking, but where other plants may prove difficult this is one which will flourish. The outstanding variety is the hybrid Warley Rose, a dwarf shrublet bearing rich carmine-pink flowers throughout summer. Earlier in bloom is *A. iberideum* which bears white flowers and silvery-grey foliage. Another dainty species is *A. kotschyanum* which covers itself in a mat of silvery-pink flowers. Where the soil is lacking in humus, the aethionemas will do well.

ANDROSACE. Several species of this plant will thrive in a chalky soil; in fact they all prefer some limestone chippings placed round their crowns and a small quantity of lime worked into the soil. *A. carnea*, with its neat habit and fleshy-pink flowers in bloom late in spring, is a lovely plant, whilst *A. carnea laggeri* bears deeper coloured flowers. *A. chamaejasme*, the dwarf jasmine, bears white flowers with yellow centres during mid-summer. Flowering well into autumn is *A. lanuginosa*, which bears hairy green leaves and bloom of pale lavender with an attractive red eye. Another of charm is *A. villosa* which produces its clusters of white flowers during spring. All the androsaces require a gritty, well-drained soil.

CHEIRANTHUS. No alpine is lovelier in early summer than the dainty double yellow wallflower of dwarf habit, *C. cheiri*, which loves lime and a poor, hot soil. A new dwarf bright orange variety called Rufus is equally lovely, whilst Keeling's Variety opens pink and bronze.

CYCLAMEN. See Chapter 15.

DIANTHUS. These are the great chalk-loving plants quite indispensable on the rockery whatever its situation, though they do prefer a sunny position. Like the primulas, the selection is vast and a whole book could well be devoted to the subject. But here are just a few lovely varieties and species. *Dianthus alpinus* bears its large rose-pink flowers amidst rich grey-green foliage during May and June. A very lovely new dianthus is named Dainty Maid, the single crimson blooms having a distinct white edge.

Neat in habit is the double crimson Mars being delightfully clove scented. Superb also is Elizabeth which bears double pink flowers with a brown centre. Flowering throughout summer is Fusilier which covers itself in a mass of single scarlet blooms, whilst Little Jock bears double flowers of delicate apple blossom pink. Of the species, *D. microlepis* grows only 1″ high, the minute pink flowers being in scale with tiny leaves. An interesting flower is *D. squarrosus* with its laciniated flowers of purest white borne above mounds of grey foliage. Then there is *D. deltoides Bizarre* which bears tiny pink flowers, striped white, and *D. granticus* Huntsman with its masses of deep scarlet flowers. There are many more but those mentioned will be found most interesting.

ERICA. It is the carnea varieties that will tolerate lime, the three best being King George, deep salmon-pink, W. T. Rackliffe, white, and Vivelli, crimson. They are winter flowering and should be given some peat in the soil.

GERANIUM. So long as they are given a sunny position and a well-drained soil on the poor side, the geraniums will thrive in a lime soil. *G. farreri* is the first to bloom, in May, its large, flat flowers of pale lavender being most attractive. Flowering early and over a long season is *G. subcaulescens*, its deep pink flowers having black centres whilst the foliage is pale sage-green. Mid-summer flowering is *G. argenteum* which has silver foliage and pink flowers, veined cerise-pink. *G. cinereum purpureum* bears rich pink blooms, whilst its white companion, album, is even lovelier. All will grow readily and true from seed.

Geranium sub-caulescens

GYPSOPHILA. All the gypsophilas thrive in a lime-laden soil and none more so than the trailing *G. repens* Letchworth Variety which bears masses of deep-pink flowers from May to August. Another with trailing habit is the shell-pink flowered *G. fratensis*, whilst the new *G. nana* is an interesting plant, being of cushion habit and studded with almost stemless white flowers.

IRIS. See Chapter 15.

OMPHALODES. Although these plants favour a partially shaded position, they are tolerant of lime and so are included here. 87

Flowering from March until May is *O. verna* which bears sprays of sky-blue flowers like forget-me-nots, but an even better plant is *O. luciliae* which flowers from June to September. Its grey foliage and sprays of purest lavender-blue produce a charming effect. The cuttings will easily root in a sandy soil, but when planted on the rockery give them liberal amounts of lime rubble.

PETROCALLIS. This is an alpine plant from the Pyrenees which will flourish in a chalk soil. It forms a cushion which during early summer becomes covered with a mass of sweetly perfumed lavender flowers.

POLYGALA. Though they love some peat or leaf mould in the soil, the polygalas are quite happy in a chalky soil, especially *P. calcarea* which bears its rich blue flowers during early summer. The flowers are shaped like those of the broom and are most attractive amidst their glossy-green leaves like those of the box. In fact the species *P. chamoebuxus* is known as the dwarf box. It likes a sunny position where it will soon make a large plant, its cream and bronze flowers being most attractive. Rarely exceeding a height of more than 4″, *P. vayredae*, a native of Spain, is of similar habit and bears flowers of a rich crimson colour during May.

RAMONDA. See Chapter 11.

SAXIFRAGA. Quite a number of saxifrages of all sections will flourish in a chalky soil, especially those of the Engleria or Encrusted Section. Many of the others are described in Chapter 11, but here we may mention some of those of the Encrusted Section, which like a dry soil and position of full sun. This section comprises some of the loveliest plants of the rock garden, none being lovelier than Tumbling Waters which produces long white sprays often 2′ in length. As a contrast in size the aizoon saxifrages form compact little mats only 3″ high, lutea being pale yellow; rosea, deep pink, and Rex, pure white. Then there is the lovely hybrid Dr. Ramsay, its white flowers being heavily dotted deep crimson, whilst Esther forms compact rosettes and long sprays of sulphur yellow. Equally lovely is *S. sendtneri* which produces large rosettes and sprays of shell-pink over a long period.

88   SCABIOUS. We know well the scabious as being one of our

most popular flowers for cutting and of its great liking for lime. The alpine species are of course not suitable for cutting, yet equally lovely and they also have a large appetite for lime. A delightful little plant is *S. alpina* which throughout summer bears its tiny heads of pale mauve flowers. Then there is *S. lucida* which bears its pale pink bloom right into autumn and *S. graminifolia* with its attractive silver-green foliage and deep violet flowers. Equally as charming is *S. Columbaria* which bears its pale blue heads during May and June. All appreciate a dressing of lime every autumn and they should be increased by division in March rather than in autumn just like their bigger brothers.

SILENE. Known as the Catchfly plant owing to the sticky substance on the leaves of serveral varieties giving the plant the ability to catch flies. A well-drained soil in full sun suits this plant the best. The plants of all species are very compact, making most of them suitable to plant between paving stones. They flower throughout early summer, but just one species, *S. keiskii*, which should be given cloche protection during winter, will bloom from July until October. Producing tiny cushions and wee star-like white flowers is *S. acaulis alba*, whilst the variety *S. saxatilis* covers itself with masses of pink flowers. Different in its requirements in that it prefers a shaded rockery is *S. alpestris* which bears taller stems covered with starry white blooms. Suitable for a rockery made by the seashore, where salt spray and a sandy soil suit it admirably, is *S. maritima*, also white flowered, but there is also a double form, very beautiful. One of the few of the silenes to bear a coloured flower is *S. schaftae*, a native of the Caucasus which bears rosy-lavender flowers, often right into late autumn.

SISYRINCHIUM. Though generally described as being suitable to any ordinary soil, I have found that this plant, the 'blue-eyed grass', will flourish in a soil containing some lime. But it must have a sunny position, for the flowers which are borne at the end of grass-like leaves do not open in the shade. Ball's Mauve, with deep purple flowers and a dainty habit is perhaps the best, but *S. bermudianum* which blooms almost the whole year round is also excellent. As a contrast *S. boreale* bears yellow flowers.

89

Polygala chaemaebuxus

Silene schafta

SOLDANELLA. These dainty little plants should be given scree conditions and a soil containing plenty of lime. If planted in a dry, sunny area, such as in East Anglia, they should be given partial shade. In the North they will be happy anywhere though should be covered with a cloche or sheet of glass during winter, not to protect them against the cold, but to give shelter from excessive moisture. The plants, which do not exceed 3″ in height, come into bloom very early in spring. One of the loveliest is *S. alpina*, with its tufts of round green leaves and nodding violet bells. Equally lovely is *S. pindicola* which bears bells of rich lavender, whilst *S. minima* appears as a carpet of pale lilac tubers which are veined with purple inside. *S. montana* has a slightly taller habit and bears many rich lavender-mauve bells which have attractive frilled petals.

Soldanella montana

Alyssum saxatile,
Aubrietia & Tulip Oriental
Splendour

13 Plants for a Sun-baked Rockery

Here the choice is great for these natives of the Mediterranean and other warm areas revel in hot, dry conditions provided they are given a soil containing some humus.

ACHILLEA. These little aromatic plants, like most herbs, are at their best on a sandy soil and in a position of full sun. One of the loveliest is *Achillea argentea* with its silvery foliage and flat, white flower heads. A magnificent plant, too, is *A. rupestris* which grows to a height of only 6″ and produces its large white umbels from green feathery foliage. *A. tomentosa* produces neat heads of golden-yellow, whilst the form *lewisii*, of similar colouring, is of even daintier habit and remains in bloom from May until October; an indispensable member of the rock garden.

ALYSSUM. Gold Dust, as *Alyssum saxatile* is called, is known to us all for it provides a superb golden contrast to the aubrietias during early summer. There are other varieties even lovelier; one is called Dudley Neville of compact habit with the flowers of a rich shade of cream, whilst *flore pleno* is later flowering and fully double, producing a very rich effect. These alyssums will flourish in as dry and as baked a position it is possible to find for them.

ANTHEMIS. More popularly known as chamomile with its aromatic foliage, the dainty *A. aizoon* is well suited to the rockery, reaching a height of only 6″ and bearing its pure white heads from its feathery silver foliage.

ANTIRRHINUM. Yes, there are several lovely alpine species of this well-known bedding plant which flower from June until October. Perhaps the loveliest species is *A. asarina* with its grey hairy leaves and cream flowers like a miniature snapdragon. A charming evergreen species *A. sempervirens* is even more dainty, its creamy flowers being small but freely produced.

AQUILEGIA. One of my favourites amongst all rockery plants, they should be planted as freely as space permits. Superlative is *A. alpina Hensol Harebell* with its rich purple bells, a plant which will come true from seed. All the aquilegias will come fairly true from seed and so are easily raised in this way from seed sown in spring. A rare, but easily cultivated species is *A. Bertoloni* which bears its blue and white flowers on but 3″ stems. The scarlet and golden blooms of *A. canadensis* are also outstanding on the rockery and if possible plant them with the dark crimson-flowered *A. rubicunda*. A magnificent species is *A. scopularum* which produces its large spurred flowers of sky blue on 3″ stems from June to September.

ARABIS. So common did *A. albida* with its grey foliage and masses of pure white flowers become, that the arabis has recently been looked upon to be more useful for covering an unsightly bank than to be planted alongside more refined plants on the rockery. There are, however, a number of charming species with a neat and equally free-flowering habit which should not be neglected. One is *A. coccinea* which bears masses of red flowers throughout summer, the plant rarely reaching a height of more than 3″. Plant with it *A. carducharum* of similar habit but bearing white flowers. *A. sundermannii* bears rich rose-coloured flowers on equally dwarf stems.

ARTEMISIA. This is the Wormwood of the herb garden with its aromatic foliage and shrub-like habit. Few of them rarely exceed 6″ in height and several remain evergreen throughout the year. *A. rupestris* bears its tiny yellow flowers amidst its deep-green foliage, whilst *A. pedemontant* produces a wealth of silver-green foliage. For planting with the dwarf evergreen cupressus trees, plant *A. villarsi* which will reach a height of 16″ and looks like a silver cupressus tree. Its foliage is strongly aromatic.

AUBRIETIA. Easily the most popular of all rock plants for the dry wall, paving and for the rockery. The aubrietias will grow almost anywhere but love best a sunny position and a soil containing plenty of humus. Wall or Rock Cress, as it is called, will bloom from April until mid-summer and will quickly form a large clump with its semi-trailing habit which should be kept tidy by trimming after it has flowered. Aubrietia is easily raised from seed but the named varieties should be propagated either by layering or from cuttings. Varieties are numerous, there must be at least a hundred, but some of the largest flowered and of the most outstanding colours are:

CARNIVAL. Rich deep purple.
GLORIOSA. Large silver-pink.
KELMSCOT GEM. Double brilliant scarlet.
KELMSCOT WONDER. Double purple.
LILAC TIME. Lovely lilac-mauve.
MRS. J. BAKER. Lavender-blue with distinct white eye.
RED CARNIVAL. Bright crimson-red.
RUSSELL'S CRIMSON. Rich wine-red.
STUDLAND. Lavender-blue, a beauty.

CALCEOLARIA. For a warm, sunny rockery and a dry sandy soil there are a number of charming species which are of great interest on the rockery. Requiring winter protection does *C. darwinii* which bears deep orange flowers of the familiar calceolaria form, each bloom having a white band round the front. Also flowering in July is *C. arachnoidea* which bears pale purple blooms. Earlier to bloom is *C. sinclairii* which bears its white, spotted red blooms on 6" stems. Of dwarfer habit is *C. biflora* later to bloom and which produces brighter yellow flowers.

CAMPANULAS. See Chapter 11.

DIANTHUS. See Chapter 12.

ERODIUM. Known as Heron's Bill and a member of the geranium family. Their great value is their long-flowering season, most of them being in bloom from May until October. Of almost prostrate habit they are useful plants for paving. One of the best is *E. reichardi roseum*, the green rosettes being studded with pink flowers and of which there is an attractive double form. Interesting is *E. guttatum* which bears white flowers on 6" stems, the blooms being blotched chocolate colour. Bearing stemless flowers of deep pink is the almost prostrate *E. corsicum* and its white counterpart album.

FUCHSIA. On the rockery situated close to the sea or in the South-West where hard frosts are rarely experienced, the fuchsia may be grown without fear of frost damage. Elsewhere it may be damaged during a severe winter though cloche protection may prevent this. One of the hardiest is a hybrid called Tom

Thumb which forms a neat little bush about 8″ high and covers itself with pretty carmine and purple tassel-like flowers throughout summer. Of similar habit is *F. pumila* which bears scarlet and purple flowers. The most dwarf of all is *F. procumbens*, its rich green leaves being formed along the ground, its green and golden blooms on sturdy 3″ stems. These fuchsias are valuable in that they remain in bloom from June until October.

GERANIUM. See Chapter 12.

GEUM. The geums are included in this chapter though they will grow anywhere, even in heavy shade, but it is only in full sun that they produce their richest colourings. The first to bloom is *G. montanum* which bears the first of its stemless bright yellow flowers in May. This is followed by *G. reptans*, also golden flowered. For a contrast and continuing in bloom into November is the rich orange *G. rivale* which is really happiest in moist, shady places. Its little nodding flowers are most quaint.

HELIANTHEMUM. Now grown in almost as large quantities and in as great a number of varieties as the aubrietias, this is a grand plant for a hot, dry soil, in bloom from mid-June until late in August. The plant has an added attraction in its shiny, dark-green leaves which are held secret on strong wiry stems and which are evergreen.

It is *Helianthemum vulgare* and its numerous varieties that are so colourful and like the aubrietia there must be almost a hundred varieties. Some of the loveliest are:

BEN ATTOW. Lemon-yellow.
BEN DEARG. Salmon-red.
BEN LAWERS. Tangerine, shaded lemon.
BEN LEDI. Rich crimson.
FIREBALL. Double scarlet.
JUBILEE. Double yellow flushed orange.
SNOWBALL. Double pure white.
ST. JOHN'S COLLEGE. Deep golden-yellow.
WATERGATE ROSE. Deep salmon-pink.
WISLEY PRIMROSE. Grey foliage, pale yellow.

Of the other species, *H. alpastre* with prostrate foliage covers itself with yellow blooms, whilst *H. umbellatum* is taller growing and bears icy-white flowers early summer. All are readily increased from cuttings.

HELICHRYSUM. It is not realized by many that there are several dainty little everlasting flowers suitable for the rockery. *H. bellidioides* bears attractive white flowers on 6″ stems, whilst *H. frigidum* reaches a height of only 2″ and also bears tiny white flowers. A very pretty species, bearing sprays of golden flowers is *H. thianschianicum*.

IBERIS. With their glossy evergreen foliage and flat heads of lilac and white flowers, these are most valuable members of a sunny rockery. They are readily increased from cuttings and are quite hardy. The variety, Little Gem, flowering in May, makes a compact little bush, whilst *I. jordani* of prostrate habit is suitable for crazy paving. Both these bear clear white blooms, but *I. Gibraltarica* bears large mauve flowers and also blooms a month earlier.

LEWISIA. These lovely plants are amongst the most beautiful of the rockery and given a sun-baked position and a good loamy soil will produce their interestingly striped flowers during June and July. The leaves are succulent, the roots fleshy, and so though liking a hot sunny position they must have a soil which will retain moisture during summer. The most outstanding variety is *L. cotyledon*, Howell's Variety, which bears rosettes of thin long leaves and on 9″ stems its large blooms of rich apricot, striped with salmon-pink. Another lovely species is *L. heckneri*, its blooms being pink, striped with white. All are natives of Columbia and Oregon, and as a contrast plant *L. columbiana* which bears sprays of richly striped purple flowers and is of dwarf habit.

LINARIA. Liking a dry, sandy soil, few alpine plants are more free flowering than the dwarf flaxes, nor of more easy culture. *L. aequitriloba*, almost the smallest of all alpines, bears tiny lavender-blue flowers, but perhaps more arresting is *L. alpina*, the violet flowers having a vivid orange lip. The variety *L. rosea* bears bloom of a clear pink. *L. organifolia* covers itself with tiny violet flowers and *L. hepaticifolia* bears its shell-pink blooms on stems which appear as much as several feet away from the plant.

LUPIN. We all know the stately border lupins but two most 95 charming dwarf species make ideal plants on the rockery; one is *L. lyallii* which bears tiny spikes of pale blue, the other is *L. ornatus*, similar in colour but with silvery leaves and both come true from seed.

NIEREMBERGIA. A native of the mountain ranges of South America, these tiny shrubs cover themselves with campanula-like blooms from May to October. The loveliest is *N. caerulea* which bears deepest violet flowers which have a bright yellow centre. More dwarf is *N. rivularis* which bears white gentian-like blooms with a golden throat. Both are delightful rock plants.

OENOTHERA. Known as the Evening Primroses for their primrose-yellow blooms open at sundown, there are several charming alpine species apart from the biennial we know so well. They love a warm, sunny position where they will flourish. One of the loveliest of them all is *O. acaulis* which bears large stemless flowers of a delicate pink shade. Bearing blooms of the familiar pale yellow shade is *O. macrocarpa*, of trailing habit which flowers late in summer, whilst of similar habit and later to bloom is *O. fremontii*, all of them bearing flowers at least 3" in diameter.

ONOSMA. Evergreen perennials with grey, hairy foliage and bearing long tubular flowers having the delicate fragrance of almonds, the onosmas are amongst the loveliest plants of the alpine garden in flower during May and June. Perhaps the loveliest of all is *O. echioides*, known as the Golden Drop Plant, the pale yellow tubes hanging in bunches and remaining quite indifferent to wind and rain. *Onosma cassia* bears a similar shaped bloom of purest white borne on hairy stems, whilst *O. siehiana* bears pink and crimson blooms through June and July.

PHLOX. These charming plants with their semi-trailing habit and their great freedom of flowering should be on every rockery. They are happy anywhere but never more brilliant than in full sun. There are two chief species *P. douglassii* and its hybrids, May Snow, producing sheets of brilliant white, and Violet Queen, with its purple-blue flowers. The habit of this species is almost prostrate and may be used amidst crazy paving. Slightly more erect in growth is *Phlox subulata* and its numerous hybrids,

96

their brilliantly coloured starry flowers held well clear of the mat-like foliage. One of the loveliest is Betty, rich salmon-pink; Sampson, rich rose-pink; whilst G. F. Wilson is a lovely clear lavender shade and Temiscaming a brilliant crimson of compact habit. A recently introduced species, of branching habit in bloom before those mentioned in early spring, is *P. stolonifera* Blue Ridge, which produces spires of lovely sky blue.

POTENTILLA. Of shrubby habit and producing their brilliant flowers over a long period, these lovely alpines revel in plenty of sunshine and a dry soil. There is a wide range of species, but those with a dwarf compact habit should be chosen for the rockery. Charming is the tiny *P. ambigua* which bears its golden flowers all summer. Equally lovely is *P. aurea flore pleno*, a golden yellow of double form. *P. mandschurica* is outstanding, its pure white blooms held above its grey foliage, whilst equally charming is *P. tonguei* with its apricot and scarlet flowers. Most compact of all is *P. nitida Alannah*, its silvery carpet foliage being covered with starry pink flowers.

ROSE. Delightful plants for the rockery, or for trough garden and window box are the miniature roses which make neat bushes no taller than 8″. The most dwarf is Rouletti, which bears its dainty double pink blooms at a height of only 4″. Also bearing double pink button-like blooms is Sweet Fairy, whilst Little Princess bears double white flowers; of rich colouring is Rosa Peon, crimson with white eye, and the scarlet flowered Maid Marion.

SAXIFRAGA. Encrusted Section. See Chapter 12.

SEMPERVIVUM. Equally suitable for dry wall and crazy paving, even for planting on the stone roof of house or outbuilding, the sempervivums, or House Leeks, will grow almost anywhere, even in an almost soil-less situation. There is a wide choice of these fleshy plants which are readily increased by pulling off the tiny offsets and planting in pans or small pots of gritty compost. One of the loveliest is *S. arachnoideum, Stansfieldii* which forms beautifully webbed fleshy rosettes of pale green tinged with crimson. Another lovely form is *S. ruthenicum* which bears fleshy deep green leaves tinged with crimson, whilst *S. atropurpureum* bears large bronzy-purple leaves. As a contrast *S. atlanticum* bears bright green rosettes and *S. cornutum* those

Phlox subulata-Betty

of a yellow-green colour. *S. arenarium* is an unusual species, forming tiny vivid green star-like rosettes in abundance which show up vividly on a scree. *S. kosaninii* is an interesting plant, the rosettes being almost flat and tipped red, the flowers carried on 6″ stems being crimson edged with white. The true House Leek is *S. tectorium* which bears large, thick, rich green pointed leaves, tipped purple.

THYMUS. See Chapter 8.

VERBENA. Not quite hardy in the coldest part of Britain, the verbenas should be covered with a cloche during winter. All are of such striking colourings that they should be grown in favourably situated gardens. Outstanding with its grey leaves and rich violet flower heads is *V. tenera Mahoneti*, a native of the Argentine and in bloom throughout summer. Plant with it *V. chamaedrifolia*, of prostrate habit and bearing its vivid scarlet heads right to the end of October. These verbenas are best lifted in late October and cuttings taken for propagation in the alpine house.

ZAUSCHNERIA. The species *Z. californica* is a superb plant for the dry rockery and the most colourful autumn alpine. Propagated by division, it bears flaming orange-red blooms held above its grey-green foliage, a single plant providing a brilliant effect when the rockery is beginning to look somewhat bare.

A Kentish rock garden

14   Plants for an Acid Soil

The great value of a rockery is that no matter how acid is the
soil there is a wide selection of suitable plants which will
provide colour throughout the season. It will be found that
most plants liking an acid soil will also be happy in shaded
places and so the two go hand in hand, for it is most often
found that the soil in a shaded situation is of an acid nature.
Such plants will flourish in the moist dell garden, plants like
the bog primulas, the dicentra and the corydalis, and here the
soil should be allowed to remain in its natural state for it
should contain ample supplies of natural humus. If it is

required to neutralize the excessively acid soil of one alpine garden, then a quantity of lime should be worked in and those plants happy in a neutral or only slightly acid soil should be used. Those requiring a really acid soil should be planted in the woodland garden.

ANDROMEDA POLIFOLIA. This is a dainty little evergreen shrub liking an acid soil but as much sunshine as possible. The shell-pink little bells are borne above the shiny green leaves during early summer.

ANEMONE HEPATICA. Loving a moist semi-shaded position and a slightly acid soil, this lovely anemone greatly resents disturbance and should be planted where it may be left alone. A dainty plant, producing its rich mauve flowers on 6″ stems early in April it is now usually catalogued as *Hepatica triloba*.

ASTILBE. A cool moist, acid soil and some shade are the requirements of this plant and what a lovely thing it is. *A. crispa* bears feathery red foliage and spires of rose-pink during August, whilst *A. simplicifolia* bears its plumes of pale salmon-buff during June. The tiniest of all is *A. saxatilis* which bears its neat spires of palest pink during mid-summer.

CALCEOLARIA TENELLA. This is a plant of creeping habit that could well be used amidst crazy paving though it likes an acid soil and one containing some peat. In such a soil it will throw up its minute slipper-like flowers throughout summer, on stems no higher than 2″.

CALTHA. These are tiny species of the familiar Marsh Marigold which prefer a damp, partially shaded place and a slightly acid peaty soil. *C. palustris flore pleno* is the buttercup we all know but in an attractive double form, whilst *C. leptosepala* bears white buttercup-like flowers during May and June. With creeping habit and equally useful about crazy paving as on the rockery is *C. sagitta*, one of the few alpines to bear a green flower.

CASSIOPE. Evergreen and fond of plenty of peat in the soil, several of the species are delightful early summer flowering plants, none being more lovely than *C. fastigiata* with its nodding white bells, whilst even more dwarf is *C. selaninoides* with its moss-like foliage and tiny white nodding bells.

100   CELMISIA. There are several species which like a slightly acid

soil, but a reasonably dry, sunny position. They are like dwarf Cosmeas, having feathery foliage and flowers like small marguerites. The best is *C. sessiliflora* with its yellow-green foliage and large, pure white flowers in mid-summer.

CYPRIPEDIUM. The lovely Lady's Slipper orchids are amongst the finest of shade-loving alpines. They like a well-drained, acid soil and will be quite happy in almost complete shade. But they must be given plenty of humus in the soil. They all bloom in May and amongst the best is *C. acaule*, which bears a dainty slipper-like bloom of brown with a pouch of deep pink on 6" stems, making it the most dwarf of all the cypripediums. Equally lovely is *C. macranthus* which bears a bloom of white veined with crimson. In the woodland garden planted by the side of stone steps they look enchanting.

DABOECIA. These are dainty heather-like plants in bloom from June until October and quite happy in either full sun or partial shade. The most suitable for the rockery is *D. azarica* which bears large nodding heather bells of rich crimson. *D. polifolia* is charming, but flowers on 15" stems and is happier in the woodland garden. It bears handsome purple bells, and as a contrast *D. polifolia alba*, pure white, is equally lovely.

DICENTRA. Happy in any position shielded from the sun and in a moist, peaty soil, these are superb little hooded plants for the rockery. The two most suitable alpine species both have blush-white flowers and silvery-grey foliage. *D. cucullaria* and *D. oregona* have similar habit, but the former blooms during spring and *D. oregona* is in bloom early in summer. Possibly lovelier than either is *D. pusilla* with an almost prostrate habit and bearing lovely rose-coloured flowers. *D. formosa* is also a lovely plant producing dainty sprays of rich pink.

DODECATHEON. Similar to the dicentras in their love of a damp, acid soil and liking some shade, the American Cowslips, with their drooping bells like those of the Solomon's Seal, will bloom during early summer. *D. alpinum* is a charming plant having purple flowers tinged with white; whilst *D. integrifolium*, has bells of a lovely shade of pale lilac. Exceptionally dwarf and dainty is *D. pauciflorum* with its rich pink, star-like flowers so freely produced.

ERICA. The heaths which will tolerate acid conditions are   101

Caltha palustris fl.

numerous in comparison with those enjoying a lime soil. All are easily propagated by root division or by inserting the cuttings in a compost of sand and peat. They bloom from July to October, whereas the lime lovers, *Erica carnea* and varieties, bloom from Christmas until Easter. An acid-loving heath enjoying a sunny position is *E. cinerea*, the loveliest being the deep blood-red *atrosanguinea* which is of dwarf, compact habit. Plant with it a new hybrid of charm called Dawn which bears clusters of deep rose coloured flowers and a form of *E. cinerea* called Golden Hue which bears deep purple flowers.

Of *Erica vulgaris*, J. H. Hamilton, with its double salmon-coloured flowers, is a lovely plant; so is that most dwarf of all varieties, Mrs. Pat, with its silver and crimson foliage. Another excellent heather is the double white form, *alba plena*. Nor must we forget *E. vulgaris foxii nana* of tiny form and bearing little rosy-mauve globe-shaped flowers.

GAULTHERIA. Natives of the mountainous regions of Eastern countries, these little evergreen shrubs favour a distinctly acid soil, a cool, moist root system and some sun. With its prostrate habit and shiny foliage, its white flowers in June followed by red berries in autumn, *G. myrsubutes* is a delightful plant for the trough garden and rockery. Another lovely species is *G. adenothrix* which bears large pinky-white flowers, also followed by bright red berries, whilst the almost prostrate *G. trichophylla*, which has rich green foliage and pink flowers followed by attractive, light blue berries in autumn, is also a charming little shrub.

GENTIAN. The gentians are such a huge race that there are species suitable for almost every soil and situation. Those described in Chapter 11 love a cool, northerly aspect and an acid-free soil, but there is a wide range of species which will flourish in a moist, acid soil either in sun or partial shade. Of these *G. altaica* bears a rich navy-blue tubular flower, in bloom during early summer, whilst *G. geargii* bears its green and purple bell-shaped blooms during early autumn. A very lovely gentian is *G. newberryi*, the greeny-blue tubular flowers, spotted with deeper green inside, are freely produced throughout midsummer. So here are three gentians for an acid soil that if planted in groups of two or three will be in bloom until the end of September. But we must not leave out what is possibly the best of all gentians, *G. sino-ornato* which bears its long navy tubes 2″ in length above glossy-green rosettes from early September until December in sheltered gardens and in the utmost profusion. Propagation is by division of the roots in spring. Incredibly lovely is *G. affinis*, taller-growing and suitable for the woodland garden, for planting by the sides of steps where it will produce its small sky-blue tubes throughout late summer.

MYOSOTIS. Though great shade lovers and enjoying a moist soil, I am not too sure that the alpine species of forget-me-not like an acid soil. A rich loam containing plenty of moisture-holding humus seems to suit them well, though a slightly acid soil will do them no harm. Of tiny habit and liking the scree garden is *M. uniflora* which bears unusual lemon-coloured flowers and attractive grey foliage. *M. nummularia* definitely does like an acid soil. It is an almost prostrate shrub bearing white flowers followed by pink berries late in summer. Delightful for a trough or for growing in pans is *M. rupicola* which is of tiny compact form and bears its heads of the brightest blue. *M. alpestris*, Ruth Fischer, loves moisture in abundance and is never happier than in the bog or woodland garden where it bears its sky-blue flowers in abundance.

OXALIS. Like the species of the anemone, the oxalis may be   103 of either herbaceous or bulbous form, but all appreciate a cool, moist soil and several of them a soil of an acid nature. They are delightful plants for mixing with other more colourful plants to which the flushed white colour of the oxalis flowers act as a pleasing foil. Dainty of habit and flowering late in spring is *O. acetosella* which blooms so well in a cool, leafy soil. Liking similar conditions and bearing large lilac globes on but tiny stems is *O. adenophylla*. Liking a shaded secluded position and an acid soil is the attractive *O. enneaphylla*, a bulbous oxalis which bears its lovely pearly-white globes throughout summer.

PARNASSIA. Of the two well-known species, one *P. nubicola* prefers a rocky slope, well drained and in sun; the other, *P. palustris*, likes the damp, peaty soil of the bogs, but both prefer an acid soil. Both bear white flowers veined with green and both bear their blooms on 8″ stems above tufts of rich green leaves.

PENNETTYA. Varying in height from 2″ to 2′ it is the prostrate *P. tasmanica* which is the best plant for a rockery, its tiny nodding bells of June giving place to scarlet berries in autumn. It prefers a shady position and a soil containing plenty of peat. Plant it near a large stone where its roots can penetrate and seek summer moisture.

PHYLLODOCE. Charming plants for an acid, peaty soil and appreciating some shade, these are dainty shrublets having evergreen foliage and flowering in April. *P. aleutica* is an exceptionally pretty plant bearing small yellow bells along the stems, whilst *P. empetriformis* of almost prostrate form covers its stems with rich rose flowers. Plant with it *P. caerulea* which bears clusters of rich mauve flowers from late in March.

PRIMULA. Enjoying a slightly acid soil and the dampness of the bog garden or a soil where peat and leaf mould abounds, are the Asiatic primulas, from China, Tibet and Northern India. One of the loveliest is *P. bulleyana* which grows to a height of 2′ and bears in June its golden whorls above clumps of rich green leaves. *P. denticulata*, with its ball-shaped heads of mauve, also does well in a moist, peaty soil. Its two most striking varieties are the brilliant crimson Red Emperor and the clear white *alba*. Hay's Variety bears heads of rich rosy-mauve.

Of dwarf, sturdy habit is *P. rosea grandiflora*, its clear pink flowers being of the clearest and richest pink I know of any flower. Deliciously fragrant are the white tiers of *P. chionantha*, the smooth leaves being covered with meal. It loves a peaty, moist soil when several plants together will produce a superb effect. Another primula for shade and a moist, acid soil is *P. frondosa*, the Bird's Eye Primula, with its attractive pink flowers and bright yellow eye. This is a tiny species and valuable for trough or pan. Superb with its delicately perfumed pale yellow blooms in a damp soil in bog garden or in partial shade, is *P. sikkimensis* which flowers on 2' stems during the latter part of summer.

RHODODENDRON. See Chapter 16.

SAXIFRAGA. It is members of the Porphyrion Section which favour an acid, peaty soil and a position of some shade. Suitable for crazy paving on account of its prostrate habit is *S. oppositifolia* which bears almost stemless purple flowers above a cushion of bright green.

SHORTIA. Delightful little evergreen shrubs loving conditions of almost complete shade and in bloom late in spring, *S. grandiflora* is perhaps the best, bearing foliage which turns crimson at the edges and waxy deep pink flowers. *S. galacifolia* bears glossy green foliage and waxy white bells in profusion. Both are readily increased from cuttings.

THALICTRUM. These are plants of great charm, the flowers being borne above dainty fern-like foliage. They love a cool, moist soil when they will make a delightful display during June. The daintiest species is *T. kiusianum* which bears clusters of bright mauve flowers. Even more attractive is *T. alpinum* which bears yellow tasselled flowers on 6" stems amidst tufts of fern-like foliage. Plant with it *T. tuberosum* which is similar in habit and which produces interesting milky-white tassels.

TIARELLA. The Foam Flower is a most attractive and valuable plant on the rockery for indeed they produce their creamy-white spikes throughout summer. They are rather like the tiny spiraeas, the blooms being of a feathery nature and held on 9" stems. 105

Primula frondosa

Trillium grandiflorum

The best is *T. wherryi* which has a longer flowering season than the others.

TRILLIUM. Natives of the Canadian Rocky Mountains, the trilliums are lovely plants for a woodland rockery, bearing their blush-white flowers above shining green foliage during early summer. One of the loveliest species is *T. grandiflorum*, its blooms being large and as if polished. More dwarf of habit is *T. undulatum*, the blooms being of a clearer white, the green leaves more pointed. The plants must be given plenty of peat or leaf mould.

TROLLIUS PUMILUS. This is a dear little plant from the foot of the Himalayan Mountains producing its yellow global flowers held above bright green leaves. It loves a moist soil, either neutral or acid, but it prefers a sunny position to one of shade.

VINCA MINOR. This little evergreen plant bearing its pretty star-shaped flowers throughout summer is most valuable for any shady corner or position on the rockery and it is quite happy in an acid or neutral soil. The best variety is Bowle's Variety which bears large purple-blue flowers. Plant with it *Vinca alba*, the pure white form. Also attractive is the variegated form with its golden leaves, whilst there is also a pink form of great beauty.

VIOLET. I always feel that the violet is a flower of the cut flower grower rather than of the rock garden. They do, however, provide a pretty display throughout spring when planted in the woodland garden, left to hide their dainty form behind a stone or beneath a step of crazy paving. They thrive in a leafy soil containing a little well-rotted compost. The runners will root themselves like strawberries and may then be removed and replanted. There are a number of lovely varieties which carry the true violet perfume and I am particularly fond of the icy-coloured White Czar. The deep pink, *Coeur d'Alsace*, of very dwarf habit, is also charming, whilst the best purple variety is the well-known Czar. A variety of outstanding beauty is called Irish Elegance, which is of a rich apricot colour and is very free flowering.

15   Bulbs on the Rock Garden

There is a tendency to neglect altogether the many delightful bulbs which may be left undisturbed and will bloom in all their glory year after year, and often at a time when there is little colour on the rockery. They are mostly quite inexpensive, quite happy in full sun or partial shade and will stand up to adverse weather to a degree only equalled by the hardiest of alpine plants. Their neat habit, too, makes them ideal plants for the small rock garden, whilst labour in keeping tidy is far less than with ordinary alpines. I have recently constructed a small alpine garden composed of nothing but the small bulbous plants and I have been amazed at their all-year-round colourings.

Small rockery bulbs like a compost containing ample quantities of peat or leaf mould and a little of that slow acting fertilizer, bone meal, worked into the soil. Most of them are quite happy on a rockery facing north and given the protection of the stones about which they should be planted in drifts of half a dozen bulbs. Take care not to plant more than 2″ deep, for the small bulbs resent too deep planting. And do try to have a continuous display of colour rather than one big splash of colour in spring. As I write this in November with the rain beating down and a strong east wind blowing the spray from the North Sea across the garden, the rockery is bright with the purple of *Crocus longiflorus*, their long tubes, richly scented, being quite as colourful and even more welcome during the dark November days than the blooms of the spring-flowering species. So let us begin with the Crocus, the autumn-flowering species.

CROCUS. *Autumn flowering*. This is quite a separate race of plants to the Autumn Crocus, the *Colchicum* or Meadow Saffron which bloom during October and whose rather coarse foliage which follows the bloom makes them more suitable for the woodland than for the rock garden. In bloom from mid-

September, when the rockery is becoming a little devoid of colour, is *C. nudiflorus*, its lilac tubes appearing before the leaves. To follow in October comes *C. speciosus* with its various shades of mauve, the bulbs being so cheap that they should be planted lavishly. For November, *C. longiflorus*, also coloured violet and lavender, must not be left out for it remains long in bloom. Plant with it *C. ochroleucus*, white with a rich golden throat and one of the few of the autumn-flowering crocus not to be purple coloured. To flower right up to the year end we have *C. asturicus*, the blooms being an attractive glossy violet colour. Then from Christmas until early February, *C. laevigatus* pushes its starry flowers through the snow in the winter sunshine and remains in bloom until *C. ancryensis* comes into bloom in February and we welcome its deep orange flowers as a welcome change from the purples of autumn. Also quite inexpensive is *C. aureus*, with its glistening golden-yellow cups and which follows in March, when we also have *C. biflorus* with its white and mauve striped tubes and *C. chrysanthus* and its several lovely hybrids, of which E. A. Bowles, yellow, and the bronze-coloured Zwanenberg are outstanding.

Flowering throughout spring is *C. susianus* with its cups of orange and brown; and *C. Sieberi*, perhaps the loveliest of them all with its golden throat and blue petals. During March and April come the Dutch hybrids we know so much better. Thus we may have colour from the Crocus for almost eight months of the year and yet they are so much neglected.

ANOMATHECA CRUENTA. Still widely known under this title, the proper name is *Lapeirousia cruenta*. This delightful little montbretia-like plant bears its salmon-red flowers on 5″ stems during late summer. Though a native of South Africa, it seems to be completely hardy on all but the most exposed rockeries. If left undisturbed in the shelter of a stone it will increase rapidly.

CALOCHORTUS. Natives of the Western Coast of America, these delightful plants are lovely in the alpine lawn or on the rockery. They like moisture at flowering time which is early summer, but over winter they like as dry a position as possible. The little cup-shaped blooms are borne on 6″ stems and none is lovelier than *C. amabilis* which bears branching stems of   109 clear yellow flowers. *C. amoenus*, equally charming, bears pale pink flowers and *C. lilacinus*, tiny flowers of palest blue.

CHIONODOXA. These charming little plants are a 'must' on every rockery. They bloom during March and what a glorious splash of colour they make, especially lovely planted amongst the *Erica carnea* heathers. Most charming is *C. gigantea* with its clear blue flowers like tiny montbretias and mix with it the white form, *alba*. Then *C. sardensis* produces its tiny sprays of purest blue and equally charming is *C. luciliae*, blue with a showy white eye. There is also a lovely rose-pink form, Rosea. The chionodoxas increase rapidly, if left undisturbed, both by offsets and self-sown seed.

CYCLAMEN. These little chaps too, rather more expensive, love some shade and, like the iris, some lime in the soil, lime rubble if possible. In the semi-shaded alpine garden, where they can be left undisturbed for years, they are charming plants. The summer and autumn-flowering plants are the most inexpensive. *C. europeum*, flowering in early August, is superb and in September comes *C. neapolitamum* with its rose-pink butterfly-like blooms and silvery mottled foliage, a real delight.

Cyclamen neapolitanum

For October, plant *C. cilicicum* which bears pink and crimson blooms.

Often in bloom at Christmas is *C. Atkinsi*, expensive but lovely, resembling *C. neapolitanum* with the variety *album* pure white, exceedingly lovely. Flowering from January to

Cyclamen repandum

Iris danfordiae

Iris histrioides

Narcissus cyclamineus

March does *C. coum*, a glorious plant with its glossy green foliage and brilliant rose-coloured flowers. Then from April and into May, *C. repandum* is in bloom. As it so readily reproduces itself from seed it should be planted in the alpine lawn or in the woodland garden. Its brilliant crimson blooms and silver mottled foliage make it the most distinctive of all the hardy cyclamen and it is quite inexpensive.

111

ERANTHIS. No flower is more colourful nor so eagerly awaited than this. We know it by its golden cups set in a unique green ruff and it comes into bloom as the winter is drawing to its close. *E. hyemalis* is delightful planted on the rockery beneath dwarf conifers; so is *E. cilicica* which flowers a little later and has a bronzy ruff. Both are inexpensive and so early.

ERYTHRONIUM. Known as the Dog's Tooth Violet on account of its long pearly bulb, these are delightful plants for the well-drained rock garden, coming into bloom early in spring, their cyclamen-like flowers being fragrant and well able to stand up to the severest of weather; in fact, they prefer a northerly position. *E. dens-canis* Franz Hals with its richly-coloured flowers, like Governor Herrick violet in both colour and form, is perhaps the best, whilst there is also a pure white form called Snowflake and also the charming Pink Perfection. Expensive, but a superb plant in every way is *E. citrinum* which bears gorgeous lemon-yellow flowers on 9″ stems.

FRITILLARIA. Delightful plants for the alpine lawn or for the woodland rockery, for they are at their best only under natural conditions whilst they like a moist, peaty soil and dappled shade. Lovely is the chequered native *F. meleagris* with its nodding, purple flowers on 9″ stems. This species is at its best in the alpine lawn. For the rockery, *F. pontica* is charming, its greenish bells being tinged with rose-pink and borne on small stems, whilst for the shady rock garden, *F. thumbergi* with its delicate white bells is a delightful plant.

GALANTHUS. This, the snowdrop, should not be left out of the rockery or alpine lawn. Even planted in the pockets between crazy paving it is a most eagerly awaited sight in February. *G. elwesi*, with its grey leaves and large egg-shaped flowers, comes into bloom even through the January snows. *G. nivalis* is the snowdrop we know best, both in its single and double form. The variety *viride-apice* with deep green tipped petals is even more attractive.

IRIS. Indispensable members of the rockery, where they like a position in full sun and as dry and as well drained a soil as possible. Quite the loveliest of all the miniature irises is *I. reticulata* and its numerous hybrids. This is the 'netted' iris, so-called because of the net-like covering round the bulbs.

Some lime rubble mixed into the soil is essential for these plants. *I. reticulata* bears its lovely scented blooms in late February on but 6″ stems, the flowers being of a deep velvet-purple, the fall petals being splashed with orange. The hybrid Cantab bears a bloom of purest Cambridge blue, whilst Hercules is of an almost bronze colour, each having the familiar orange colouring on the fall petals. Very lovely is *L. danfordiae* which loves a sandy, limey soil and if given the protection of a stone will give of its rich golden blooms on the darkest of January days. Also for winter flowering there is *I. histrioides*, its rich blue flowers being spotted with black. This, too, comes into bloom during February.

In a pocket of lime rubble beneath the wall of my home, where it is surrounded by a terrace of paving stones, *I. stylosa* bears its mauve flowers all winter and neither snow nor North Sea spray seems to worry it.

For flowering in May, plant *I. sisyrinchium* which bears throughout the month a continuous display of purple and white blooms midst neat grassy foliage.

MUSCARI. The grape hyacinth should be planted as lavishly as possible for it is so inexpensive and never fails to produce its rich blue flowers in profusion. Plant it with the tiny narcissus species for they bear their yellow or white blooms at the same time and the contrast is most attractive.

Flowering by early April is *M. botryoides* Heavenly Blue and its pure white counterpart, *album*, then a little later comes *M. azureum*, of brightest blue, and later still, *M. armeniacum* and its glorious sky-blue hybrid, Cantab. All these lovely grape hyacinths are most colourful if planted in drifts of a dozen bulbs. If they have a fault it is that their thin leaves tend to become straggling long after flowering and they are better kept a little distance away from other alpine plants.

NARCISSUS. There is a wide range of charming miniature bulbs suitable for the rockery or for the alpine lawn, where they should be planted in clumps of half a dozen bulbs. They bloom on short stems and are most attractive nodding in the late spring breezes. Most dwarf of all is *N. minimus* which bears its tiny yellow trumpets on but 2″ stems, a most valuable narcissus for the small rockery. Almost as dwarf is *N. minor*, 113 both of which bloom very early in spring. Equally lovely in bloom, by the end of February in a mild winter, is *N. cyclamineus* with its yellow tube serrated at the edges and which likes a cool, moist position. It is even quite happy planted at the foot of the water rockery.

From Ireland the pretty little hybrid, Rip Van Winkle, with its narrow twisted sulphur petals tinged with green, is a most dainty plant. It is a cyclamineus hybrid, like the sweet little orange cupped Beryl which blooms in March.

A dainty narcissus of polyanthus form is *N. canaliculatus*, strongly scented, which bears three or four cupped flowers on each 6″ stem. Flowering at the same time in April, *N. bulbocodium conspicuus*, the Hoop Petticoat daffodil, is equally dwarf and likes a moist, peaty soil. In fact, this narcissus may be planted amongst plants liking an acid soil and there are several forms giving colour from early February until late in April. Nor must we leave out *N. triandrus*, the 'Angel's Tears' daffodil which produces a cluster of tiny creamy-white 'drops' which hang down from the stems like tears.

Last of the miniatures to flower is *N. juncifolius*, richly fragrant and like a tiny jonquil, borne on 4″ stems amidst its thin rush-like foliage.

SCILLA. Many of the scillas are too tall for the rockery and are better naturalized in the woodland garden. There are however three species which will, if left undisturbed, bloom to perfection on a rockery facing north and they will even tolerate a slightly acid soil. The first to bloom, late in March, is *S. sibirica* in its blue and white forms, the bells carried on but 6″ stems. To follow comes *S. pratensis*, lovely on the alpine lawn and which bears its brilliant blue bells in May, and this is followed by *S. amethystina*, of dwarf habit but bearing a large spike which will remain in bloom well into June.

TULIP. Here again, whilst we all know the early and May Flowering and Cottage tulips, those colourful little chaps so ideal for the rockery are sadly neglected. Just one will provide a display equal to a dozen of the most exotic alpine plants which is only a slight exaggeration as to their brilliance. Inexpensive and superb is *T. clusiana*, The Lady Tulip, its outer petals being cherry-red, the inner petals white. It should

114

be planted 6″ deep, preferably close to a rock. A dainty species is *T. chrysantha*, being a combination of yellow and rose.

A gem for the rockery is *T. dasystemon* which bears several flowers on a stem, coloured sulphur and on the exterior shaded grey, the flower borne on 5″ stems. Most suitable for the rockery is *T. kaufmanniana, aurea*, bearing a bloom of rich golden yellow with the outsides of the petals a vivid scarlet.

There are now a number of varieties of the species, Brilliant bearing crimson flowers with a yellow centre and Elliott white with interesting scarlet pencilling. All bear their flowers on only 6″ stems. The most dwarf of all tulips is *T. persica* which bears its flowers of yellow and bronze on but 3″ stems. It has an additional value in that it is late flowering. Nor must we omit *T. linifolia* which bears dainty blooms of vivid crimson with a striking black centre. All of them are so colourful and of such easy culture that it is strange they are not made more use of.

ZEPHYRANTHES. Several species of the Zephyr Flower are suitable for the rockery and are so valuable in that they bloom in autumn. Both *Z. candida*, with its white tubular flowers like a crocus, and *Z. rosea*, white striped rose-pink, are perfectly hardy and of dwarf habit, but provide them with a sunny position and a well-drained soil containing plenty of sand.

Tulipa linifolia

Zephyranthes candida

16 Dwarf Evergreens and Shrubs

Most important for providing the background to the rockery and trough garden are the small shrubs against which the whole colourful picture is accentuated in a most pleasing manner. Valuable for planting to provide shelter from cold winds at the sides and back of a rockery, are the taller but slow-growing conifers like the Deodar Cedar and the Blue Spruce, their attractive colourings providing a most charming frame to the picture. Plant them as freely as possible where space permits, but for the small rock garden and for planting about the stones in small groups, the tiny dwarf species are invaluable. Evergreens are so valuable in that they may be obtained in a wide range of colourings which are of course retained throughout the winter. Delightful they are, when planted with the tiny flowering bulbs, the blues of the chionodoxas, the pale yellow colourings of the miniature daffodils.

Reginald Farrer, the great authority on rock gardening of the first years of the century, has said that the correct placing of the trees and shrubs is as important as that of the rocks themselves, that indiscriminate use of the shrubs can either make or spoil the whole display. Little pines and spruces crowning the rockery will give it additional height, an important consideration for the small rock garden. Then those shrubs with a drooping habit, like the dwarf brooms, planted by a stone add to the natural effect and also provide protection for the plants loving dry conditions.

The planting of shrubs of the deciduous type should not be overdone, for their season of colour is short and they are not of such compact habit as the evergreens and the small garden should rely on the conifers with upright growth. It is advisable to plant the trees when once the stones have been placed and before any plants are set out, for it is around these trees that the rock garden takes shape. As Farrer said they are just as essential as the stones themselves. Summer planting is not advisable, for all these trees like copious amounts of water. If possible plant in the autumn or on suitable occasion over winter and see that they are never allowed to suffer from lack of moisture at all times. Some of the more dwarf species may be used not only in the trough garden or window box, but in the tiny miniature indoor gardens, planted in well-drained earthen-ware pots or pans. Planted also with a few of the winter mossy saxifrages or tiny bulbs they make an ideal table decoration when flowers are scarce and expensive.

EVERGREENS

ABIES BALSAMEA. This is the Balsam Fir which grows as broad as it does tall and rarely exceeds a height of 8". The foliage is dark green, underlined silver.

CHAMAECYPARIS. This is the large group which includes the cypress (cupressus) and retinosporas which are now most commonly used to distinguish them.

CUPRESSUS LAWSONIANA NANA. Is a tiny tree which enjoys a moist position, somewhere near the foot of the rockery. It is almost round of form and has bright green foliage. The form *ellwoodii* does not exceed a height of more than 15" and covers itself in feathery grey-green foliage.

C. FORSTECKIANA. Is another compact cypress having foliage of a lovely shade of green-grey.

C. MINIMA GLAUCA. Of globular habit, a matured tree will measure 12" high and 12" wide. The foliage is of a feathery blue-green colour, a most attractive plant.

C. CRIPPSII AUREA. Is of slightly weeping habit, its golden foliage looking more colourful planted near a stone.

RETINOSPORA OBTUSA ERICOIDES. Is also of rounded form, the foliage turning an attractive purple colour during winter.

R. OBTUSA NANA GRACILIS. One of the smallest of them all, its short, rich green branches being most attractive. The golden form *Nana aurea* has rich golden-bronze foliage.

R. PYGMAEA. A most handsome species in bronzy-green foliage, being thick and shaggy, almost spreading along the ground.

117

R. TETRAGONA AUREA. A lovely golden-yellow plant, its foliage being moss-like and dense.

R. OBTUSA HYCOPODIOIDES. Is a low-spreading form with thick branches and foliage of a bottle-green colour.

JUNIPERS. These are charming trees for the rockery, being of very slow growth with their foliage of a deep blue-grey colour.

J. COMMUNIS HIBERNICA. Is the Irish Juniper forming an upright pencil-like column of blue-grey. This form should be planted two or three together.

J. SABINA TAMARISCIFOLIA. The Carpet Juniper with a low spreading habit and with feathery tamarisk-like foliage.

J. BONIM ISLES. Another lovely spreading juniper with rich grey-blue foliage.

J. SQUAMATA MEYERI. A lovely tree having glaucous blue-grey foliage and splendid habit.

J. CHINENSIS. The Chinese Juniper of columnar form, its foliage turning a lovely mulberry shade during winter.

PICEA. This is the Spruce family, very slow and compact-growing and ideal for the rockery.

P. ALBA ALBERTINA. A delightful form of the white spruce found in Alberta and which grows only 1″ each year.

P. EXCELSA NANA COMPACTA. This is a dwarf form of the Norway Spruce, the horizontal spreading branches giving it an almost globular form.

P. EXCELSA DUMOSA. Here is an almost prostrate form of the Norway Spruce, its horizontal branches being almost at ground level.

P. EXCELSA GREGORYANA. A tiny spruce, giving the appearance of little balls of needles.

P. EXCELSA RAMONTII. Of pyramidal habit, the lower branches sitting on the ground making a tree of almost compact form and of a rich bottle green.

P. ORIENTALIS NUTANS. A little spruce having drooping branches of a shining dark green colour.

THUJA. These are delightful evergreens, most of them growing broader than they are tall and having colourful feathery foliage.

T. OCCIDENTALIS. This makes a beautiful broad tree, its feathery green foliage turning rich bronze in winter.

T. OCCIDENTALIS AUREA GLOBOSA. Even more globular in form and of a more brilliant bronze colour during autumn and winter.

T. OCCIDENTALIS OHLENDARFII. A thuja of more erect habit than the others, its foliage turning a rich shade of plum red.

TAXUS. This is the Yew in its various forms, rather more rapid growing than the other evergreens, but delightful plants for the larger rock garden.

T. BACCATA is the English Yew forming a tight dark column, a superb tree for the back of a rockery. The golden, weeping form, *dovastonii aurea*, is a most striking tree used as a specimen close to a rock.

T. CUSPIDATA NANA. Is a more slow and compact growing form, the dark branches being spreading so that the tree when fully matured can easily cover an area of 12' in diameter though attaining a height of less than 3'.

T. SEMPER AUREA. Makes a compact tree with beautiful golden foliage.

There are other suitable evergreens for the rockery apart from the conifers which may be used with advantage. Especially are the spray forms like saxifrage Tumbling Waters made more striking if planted against a background of evergreens. The following are all suitable for a rockery of average size:

Cistus x Loretti   119

AZALEA AMOENA. This is a richly coloured evergreen, the small dark green leaves turning a brilliant red-bronze in winter. Late in spring it covers itself with masses of cerise-coloured flowers.

AZALEA ROSAEFLORA. Makes a low-growing shrub, remaining green through winter and bearing a mass of rose-coloured blooms during spring.

BERBERIS BUXIFOLIA. Is similar in habit to a box, retaining its small glossy leaves and bearing pretty orange flowers in spring followed by masses of dark blue berries.

BERBERIS STENOPHYLLA. Is a shrub more for the large rockery, forming graceful arches.

CISTUS. Often called the Rock Rose, the many species are suitable for growing in dry alpine lawns or on the rockery in full sun. They are evergreen and bloom from mid-June until late in August.

C. CYPRIUS. Is a tough, long-lived plant rarely achieving a height of more than 1″, of compact habit and bearing large white flowers, spotted crimson.

C. FORMOSUS PORTUGAL. These neat bushy plants grow wild in Portugal and bear large flowers of the purest golden-yellow colour, like sovereigns.

C. INGWERSENIANUS. Of almost prostrate habit this form bears attractive pure white blooms.

C. LORETI. This makes only a tiny bush, the most compact of all, and bears large white flowers throughout summer.

C. STEANBERGI. A superb variety of almost prostrate habit, the branches being covered with masses of shell-pink flowers.

COTONEASTER CONSPICUA. This may be kept to a small bush retaining its bottle-green leaves in winter and also its orange-red berries.

COTONEASTER MICROPHYLLA. This species also retains its berries during winter. Of spreading habit it is a colourful plant for covering a stone.

EUONYMUS MINIMA. Really a climbing plant but growing no taller than 9″, is ideally suited for covering a stone to which it clings like ivy. The tiny green leaves have pretty white veins.

HEDERA MINIMA. A tiny twisted erect-growing ivy, delightful for planting near a stone in either sun or shade.

H. CONGLOMERATA. This is a prostrate form, pushing itself along the ground but being in no way troublesome.

KALMIA. *Polifolia glauca* is the Swamp Laurel, a low bush growing to a height of only about 10″. It likes a moist soil and some peat. It produces its pretty pink flowers in spring. There is a lovely prostrate form *K. mycrophylla* which bears masses of rich crimson cup-shaped flowers.

RHODODENDRON. Liking an acid, peaty soil, full sun or partial shade, the dwarf rhododendrons are charming plants. The little lavender-blue flowered hybrid Blue Tit flowering in May is a beauty, then comes *R. impeditum* with its grey leaves and rich mauve flowers in June. To bloom later in summer there is *R. ferrugineum* which bears clusters of bright carmine flowers.

Two yellow-flowering species are truly lovely, *R. caesium* and *R. campylocarpum*, both May-flowering, whilst *R. imperator* is also a charming plant growing no taller than 10″ and bearing its little purple-red bells at the same time. Another dainty species is *R. racemosum*, which is the first to bloom, producing its beautiful flesh-pink bells in early April. All are of dwarf habit and amongst the finest of all rockery plants, but remember that they do not like a lime soil.

ROSMARINUS PROSTRATUS. This is a lovely prostrate form of the Rosemary, having rich lavender flowers.

SANTOLINA NANA. This is the dwarf form of the cotton lavender with the same attractive grey foliage, pleasantly scented and bearing flowers of brightest yellow.

DECIDUOUS SHRUBS

Most of the deciduous trees and shrubs like a dry, sunny position where quite a number of them really are useful for a rockery of anything but the smallest in size.

BETULA NANA. For a specimen tree, planted close to a stone, none is lovelier than the dwarf birch, a most graceful tree which looks delightful planted close to mixed conifers.

CYTISUS. The hybrid blooms are suitable for a rockery if kept in bounds. They should be constantly checked for any decayed 121 wood and should receive constant pruning. A charming variety is the old rose coloured Enchantress, whilst *C. fuogens* covers itself in April, forming arching sprays of pale yellow.

DAPHNE. These superb early spring-flowering plants like a cool, moist soil, one containing some humus and as cool a position as possible though one sheltered from early spring winds. *D. blagayana*, which prefers some shade, is of almost trailing habit and bears its fragrant cream-coloured flowers in April. *D. collina* makes but a tiny bush and bears its rosy-red flowers in June. Of more dwarf habit than *D. mezereum* is *D. cneorum* which forms a compact cushion, completely hidden by the fragrant pink flowers during May. It likes plenty of humus in the soil and takes some little time to become established.

Daphne blagayana

GENISTA. Allied to the cytisus and also known as 'brooms', several are ideal dry soil plants and better away from excessive chalk. *G. prostata* bears little yellow sprays almost at ground level, whilst *G. decumbens*, has flowers of similar colour, the habit being almost prostrate. Both bloom early in summer and are followed by the July-flowering *G. delphinensis* which forms a mass of golden flowers. A charming plant of more upright habit is a hybrid called Peter Pan which covers itself in mid-summer with lovely bronze-crimson flowers.

122

HYPERICUM. The species *H. calycinum*, known as the Rose of Sharon, is an excellent plant to use in the shaded rock garden where it will bear an abundance of large, flat, golden-yellow blooms. *H. moserianum* is a dwarf shrub of almost prostrate habit bearing large, yellow, cupped blooms with crimson anthers.

PHILADELPHUS. There is a lovely 'mock orange' which grows no taller than 12″ and is a superb plant for a rockery. Its name is *Manteau d'Hermine* and it covers its slender branches with deliciously fragrant white flowers during July.

RIBES ALPINUM. This is the miniature form of the flowering currant, bearing pale pink flowers, but it is for its rich golden foliage that it should be included on a rockery. It will grow no taller than 10″ and remain compact without attention.

SALIX BOYDI. This tiny Willow is truly a remarkable tree, reaching a height of 10″ only after fifty years growth. This little gem makes an ideal trough or miniature garden tree, its pale green dancing foliage being most attractive. Almost as dwarf is *S. Wehrhahni*, a tiny pussy willow, covering itself with silver catkins throughout early spring.

SYRINGA MICROPHYLLA. This is a tiny Japanese lilac rarely reaching more than 18″ in height and which bears its purple sprays of bloom in early summer.

VERONICA. These shrubs do better on a seaside rockery than elsewhere. There are a number of dwarf species. *V. pageana*, with its grey leaves and creamy-white flowers, grows no taller than 10″, neither does *V. coerulea glauca*, with its blue-grey leaves and tiny spikes of pale blue.

123

Syringa microphylla

17 The Value of Annuals in the Rock Garden

Though the use of annuals for the rockery is only on a small scale, for it is far better to use perennial plants from the wide range available for all types of soil, far less work being entailed, the value of suitable annuals to cover bare patches and especially for sowing over and about early flowering bulbs to provide a continuation of colour cannot be overlooked. Besides, there are one or two annuals eminently suited to rockery work where they are more attractive than elsewhere in the garden and readily compare with other plants for beauty of colour. Take care to omit all those with a rampant, trailing habit which will tend to crowd out the plants having a more dainty habit. And those which shed their seed easily should be either avoided or confined to corners where excessive germination would not become a nuisance. But a number of annuals have a value in that they provide colour late in summer when some rockeries, though this denotes insufficient care in planning for all-year-round colour, are tending to become somewhat bedraggled. Do not attempt to use any plants which appear stiff and border-like; use only those with an alpine habit and the natural effect of the rockery will not be harmed.

AGERATUM. The little ageratums which require half hardy treatment, sowing in boxes of sandy loam in gentle heat, or in a frame for later flowering and planting out early June, are suitable subjects. Little Blue Star grows only 4″ tall and makes a rounded, compact plant; likewise, the salmon-coloured Fairy Pink. Plant with them the pure white Little Dorrit.

ALYSSUM. The hardy alyssum *minimum*, which like all hardy annuals may be sown where it is to bloom, is a useful plant. It forms a low compact plant, like a hen sitting on a nest, and covers itself with sweetly scented white flowers. The pleasing Lilac Queen, slightly taller growing, is also suitable.

ANAGALLIS. The Rock Pimpernel, producing masses of rich gentian-blue flowers. Sown round a stone they will cover it with blooms throughout summer and autumn.

ANTIRRHINUM. The bedding varieties are of course quite wrong on the rockery, but the charming Rock Hybrids have been evolved from *A. glutinosum* and grow only 6″ tall and bear masses of tiny 'snap-dragons'. They are best sown in boxes first, in gentle heat.

CANDYTUFT. Not generally regarded as a rock annual, but its habit is quite suitable and it remains long in bloom. Sown where it is to flower, the Giant White Hyacinth-flowered and the brilliant Rose Cardinal look attractive together.

CHEIRANTHUS. The mauve alpine wallflower, of compact habit, *C. linifolius*, is really a hardy biennial and should be sown in July to bloom the following spring. It is a good plant to mix with small bulbs.

CONVOLVULUS. *C. minor*, Lavender Rosette is the one to grow. It is of prostrate habit, but does not trail or climb about the rockery. Its grey foliage and pale lavender flowers make it an attractive subject which should be sown in early April.

ERINUS *alpinus* is really a perennial but is best treated as a biennial, sowing in July to bloom through the following summer. Delightful when sown between crazy-paving stones or about a dry wall.

ERYSIMUM. Another hardy biennial, but will bloom late in summer from a spring sowing bearing its bright golden-yellow blooms in profusion.

GYPSOPHILA *muralis*. How frail this little plant looks and yet how tough it really is, producing its pale pink flowers through late summer and autumn, and is a lovely subject for sowing early in spring above and around bulbs. It loves a chalky soil.

LEPTOSIPHON. Sown early in April, this dainty plant grows no taller than 6″, yet forms a large mat which it covers with flowers of various shades. It enjoys a dry, sunny position.

LIMNANTHES *douglassii*. This is a delightful hardy annual bearing its yellow and white flowers in profusion. Two sowings should be made where conditions are favourable, one in August to give colour in spring and another in April to provide late season colour.

Limnanthes Douglasii   *Mesambry anthemum criniflorum*

LINARIA *maroccana*, Fairy Bouquet is the suitable species, for the little brilliantly coloured antirrhinum-like flowers are carried on but 6″ stems. A hardy annual, this is one of the most charming of all annual alpine plants.

LINUM. The species *grandiflorum rubrum*, with its rich crimson blooms borne in profusion throughout summer, is a useful addition to the rockery, especially attractive with a limestone rock for a background.

LOBELIA. For a window box or trough, the trailing *hybrid Sapphire*, of clear blue with white eye, is a delightful plant for trailing over the sides.

MATRICARIA *eximea*. A compact plant covering itself with masses of golden balls, is most attractive on the rockery and should be given half hardy treatment.

MESEMBRYANTHEMUM *criniflorum* or the Livingstone Daisy is a half hardy plant which likes a dry, sandy soil and a position of full sun. Even planted between crazy-paving stone it will grow well, sending out its succulent claw-like foliage and covering itself in masses of the most brilliantly coloured daisies.

MYOSOTIS. Owing to its ability to reproduce itself in copious numbers, this charming plant should be confined to the more natural woodland garden or to a corner of the rockery or water garden where its reproduction will not harm other plants of more refined habit. For all that, the forget-me-not is a pleasing plant and especially of good compact habit is the variety Blue Ball, which makes a small, neat plant literally covered in navy-blue flowers.

NEMOPHILA *insignis*. Known as Baby Blue Eyes, this colourful plant with trailing habit and bright blue flowers with white eyes is most useful sown every month from April to June between crazy paving stone or about the rockery where it will provide a colourful display throughout summer.

PETUNIA. Of relaxed habit, this plant always looks quite happy on the rockery and being half hardy comes into its glorious best when colour is becoming scarce. The dwarf and brilliant scarlet Fire Chief is outstanding and though of a softer colour, Silvery Lilac is also lovely.

PHACELIA *campanularia*. This is a hardy plant that could be more often used on the rockery to advantage, for it is of compact carpet-forming habit, the navy-blue bell-shaped blooms being most attractive. It is known as the Californian Bluebell.

PHLOX DRUMMONDII. This is the half hardy phlox, the new dwarf hybrids reaching a height of only 6″ and remaining delightfully colourful right into autumn. The new variety Isabellina is of a lovely yellow shade; Meteor, salmon; and Blue Bird, sky-blue. Two or three planted together look very showy.

SEDUM *caeruleum*. This little stonecrop is of trailing form, creeping over the soil and covering itself with masses of rich blue flowers. It may be sown between paving stone as well as in crevices about the rockery stone.

SWEET WILLIAM. There is a very dwarf, compact variety of this charming old world plant that should be suitable for the rockery. It is called Indian Carpet and may be obtained in a mixture of all those lovely salmon, red, and white shades familiar to their taller cousins. They should be sown in frames in July to flower the following year.

VERBENA. With its free habit, this to my mind is just as delightful a plant on the rockery as it is for bedding. It is really a perennial but almost always given half hardy annual treatment, the seed being sown in gentle heat in March. The verbena is valuable in that it blooms right until the end of November or until the first severe frosts. Obtainable in a wide range of lovely colours and forming round heads the size of a five shilling piece, the plants should be set in groups around the stones.

Do not despise these lovely annuals. Indeed when funds were once very low, I made a most colourful rock garden by using nothing but plants which were raised from seed and the annuals took pride of place for their colour and adaptability.

621 K